Dealing with People Problems at Work

GW00802431

Dealing with People Problems at Work

Stephen Palmer and Tim Burton

The McGraw-Hill Companies

London · New York · St Louis · San Francisco · Auckland · Bogotà · Caracas
Lisbon · Madrid · Mexico · Milan · Montreal · New Delhi · Panama · Paris
San Juan · Sãu Paulo · Singapore · Sydney · Tokyo · Toronto

Published by
McGRAW-HILL Publishing Company
Shoppenhangers Road, Maidenhead, Berkshire, SL6 2QL, England
Telephone 01628 23432
Fax 01628 770224

British Library Cataloguing in Publication Data
Palmer, Stephen
   Dealing with people problems at work
   1. Interpersonal relations   2. Personnel management
   I. Title   II. Burton, Tim
   658.3'145

ISBN 0077091779

Library of Congress Cataloging-in-Publication Data
Palmer, Stephen,
   Dealing with people problems at work / Stephen Palmer and Tim
   Burton
      p.   cm.
   Includes index.
   ISBN 0-07-709177-9
   1. Supervision of employees.   2. Problem solving.   3. Employees
   – Counseling of.   I. Burton, Tim (Timothy John).   II. Title.
   HF5549.12.P35   1996
   658.3'045 – dc20   96-9254
                                                              CIP

McGraw-Hill
A Division of The McGraw·Hill Companies

12345 BL 99876

Typeset by Macreth Media Services, Hemel Hempstead, Herts.
and printed and bound in Great Britain by Biddles Ltd, Guildford and King's Lynn

Printed on permanent paper in compliance with the ISO Standard 9706.

To

Maggie, Kate and Tom

Sue, James and Eliza

Contents

Introduction

Who this book is for

This book is for anyone who routinely has to deal with people problems in the course of their work. Let's begin by unpacking that sentence.

Anyone

Anyone *means* anyone. The book makes no assumptions about:

- Where you work
- What your work involves
- Who you work with
- How you work
- What you already know about problem-solving skills
- Whether you are male, female, Black, White, with or without a disability
- What you already know about problem-solving skills

In fact, only one sort of person is absolutely not catered for by this book: the person who is unwilling to take a good hard look at their working practices and if necessary make radical changes to them. *If necessary*. After all, you may find that you are already well on the way to good practice.

So if you're not open to the possibility of a radical and overwhelmingly positive change in the way you work, you may find this book less than satisfying; but we suggest you read on all the same, and make up your mind later.

Routinely

This is important. If you only have to deal with people problems occasionally you'll find this book fairly bad value for money. But before you shut it and count the cost, think for a moment. Is encountering people problems really the exception rather than the rule? You still think so? Then ask yourself:

	Often	Sometimes	Never
● How often does my spouse/partner/dog/cat hear about my problems with people when I finish work?	☐	☐	☐
● How much time do I spend each day discussing personalities rather than tasks?	☐	☐	☐
● How often do I wake up thinking about people problems	☐	☐	☐
● How many unforeseen interruptions, in an average day, are the result of people problems?	☐	☐	☐

If your response to any of these points was 'often' or 'sometimes', then this book is for you. If all your responses were 'never', then we suggest you put your copy on one side for now, or better still, pass it to a friend or colleague who might find it useful.

Deals with

We need to be careful with this phrase. 'Deals with' doesn't mean 'sorts out'. You don't need to be a problem-solving professional to benefit from this book. In fact, if your aim is to solve other people's problems you may need to do some careful rethinking. As you work through the book you'll find that one of the most important skills we describe is helping other people solve their own problems.

People problems

First, let's clarify what we mean by 'problem'. A problem can be defined as:

● An imbalance or discrepancy between what is and what should be (i.e. conditions that are demanded or desired).

● Some obstacle or obstacles preventing the availability of an effective response for reducing this discrepancy.

In other words, we want something to change and we can't see how to bring this about. 'Dealing with' then has the goal of ensuring that this change occurs in the most positive and effective way possible.

Now let's move on to the 'people' part. We have called this book *Dealing with People Problems **at Work***. In one sense, of course, all problems are people problems. Even a malfunctioning machine part is probably malfunctioning because of a human error, or simply because of the apparently insuperable problem of making a machine work without at some point going wrong.

But here we are concerned with problems that involve:

● Communication between people
● People's experience of themselves
● People's reactions to one another

We could have called this type of problem 'emotional problems'. But one of our core convictions is that most 'emotional' problems involve thoughts as well as feelings. We could have spoken of 'communication' problems. But we want also to include the way people experience others and themselves, whether or not there is any deliberate communication going on. Finally, we could have used the term 'personal problems'; but this is too narrow and makes many people think of sexual difficulties or (even) personal hygiene! As an illustration of what we mean by people problems, here are some of the typical sorts of problem that this book is designed to assist you with.

 CASE STUDY: CYNTHIA'S COMPLAINING

Cynthia works as an assistant in a pharmacy in a large supermarket. For months she has been grousing. She began with complaints to Sue, the assistant pharmacist, about the off-duty, managing pharmacist. Then she started to complain about Anita, the dispensing assistant. All the complaints were trivial ones, but together they began to get Sue down. Morale in the pharmacy was plummeting. Sooner or later mistakes were going to be made. Customers would complain. How could Sue tackle the problem?

 CASE STUDY: ALAN'S LATENESS

Alan had been a conscientious worker in the marketing department of a small software company. Tamsin, acting head of marketing, had already noted his potential and had spoken encouragingly to him at a recent performance review. However, recently Alan had begun to arrive for work late. Initially it had been just a few minutes, but in the past week he had on two occasions turned up half an hour late, looking tired and harassed. All he had said to colleagues was 'car problems'. He wouldn't be drawn further. Tamsin suspected there was something more to it. But how could she approach Alan, given that he seemed so defensive?

 CASE STUDY: THE JOB BOMBSHELL

Riding Utilities was a large, newly privatized organization delivering essential domestic fuels to a large area of northern England. Since privatization there had been several reviews of internal organization with a view to improving competitiveness. This had resulted in growing rumours of a drastic downsizing initiative, particularly among service engineers. John Smail, service manager for the southern division, had been summoned to his divisional head's office and handed a report outlining plans that confirmed his worst fears. Although his own job seems secure he would have to reorganize his region and lay off eight of his 26 staff. How could he break the news?

The thing that all these problems have in common is that they are about the way individual staff perceive, experience, feel about their world and about each other. The issues raised are not to do with a lack of technical skill, or knowledge: they can't be solved by sending the people concerned on a conventional training course, or by referring them to a staff manual. But they can be tackled—and in many cases solved—by:

- the well-targeted application of a number of well-honed interpersonal skills
- working *with*, rather than *on*, the person concerned (we'll have more to say about this later)

At work

When we say 'at work' we mean *wherever* you work. Although the balance of case studies in this book is skewed towards medium to large size organizations, the problem-solving strategy we suggest is appropriate to anywhere that people work together. It will even be helpful to someone whose routine contact with others is by phone or e-mail. Because they, like anyone else, will encounter people problems and may be the person best placed to deal with them.

However, there is another important point we want to make about the focus of this book: people problems 'at work' may not be to do exclusively with work. They may originate elsewhere and develop into workplace problems. As a problem-solving professional you will need to be aware of potential problem areas in your colleagues' wider lives, and be prepared to include these in your remit when you meet them.

Take Cynthia's grousing, for instance. Is it really just a question of incompatible personalities at work? Probably not. How does Cynthia view her working world, and why? Maybe she expects too much of her colleagues. And maybe this is because somewhere else—at home, in her social life—someone is expecting too much of her.

Or take Alan's lateness. It could be car problems. But why is he so guarded? The possibilities are endless. Maybe he has a widowed mother who is terminally ill. He knows he will soon have to give up work to look after her. He can't face the prospect. He doesn't want it talked about at work.

And the bombshell may have wider repercussions. Breaking bad news may be a big issue for John Smail. He lives a lonely life outside of work. His self-acceptance depends on the approval of his staff. The bombshell seems to him like an act of betrayal. He feels that he'll be left friendless, desolate.

So problems at work are frequently, but of course not always, linked to wider issues that go well beyond the boundaries of the workplace. Often you will be able to help your staff tackle these. But sometimes—and it's important to be clear about this from the start—the problems your staff are caught up in will require more help than you are able to provide. We say more about this in Chapter 2.

Whose problems?

This book is intended especially for managers and supervisors who want to deal effectively with people problems at work. It outlines a straightforward menu of problem-solving skills which can greatly enhance the work performance of yourself and your colleagues. However, we need to make one thing clear right at the start. Dealing with people problems is not simply a matter of solving others' problems for them. The strategies we suggest have two other applications:

● We will provide you with a useful tool for dealing with your own problems.

Here we don't simply mean the issues people bring to you in your role as co-worker or manager. We also mean the problems that you present to others. And if you feel that you are absolutely, definitely not, no never, a source of any sort of people problem you can put this book down now, because a prerequisite for successful problem solving of any sort is personal honesty and integrity.

● We will also provide a tool with which your staff can deal with their own problems.

Really successful problem-solvers are prepared to help others to solve their own personal problems. Most of the suggestions in this book can be followed through in this way. Of course, initially your staff may look to you to suggest effective solutions. But in the longer term the solutions that really work are those that are suggested by the person presenting the problem. And surely this fits in with your overall aim as a manager? By helping your staff to gain self-help skills you will (depending on your aims) have more time to spend with more staff facing more deep-seated problems, or more time to spend on other managerial tasks essential to an efficient business.

If you want to check that we really mean business, take a quick look forward now to pp. 90–94 where we suggest ways of challenging mistaken beliefs. Note the thought form: useful for you; useful for your staff—a vital component of your multi-use problem-solving toolkit.

Finding the time to work through this book

 ACTIVITY

The list below details all the reasons why books like this tend to be put down half read. Tick those that apply to you and then read the notes that follow.
I tend not to finish books like this because:

1 I don't like the tone in which they are written. ☐
2 I haven't time. ☐
3 They don't really apply to my own work. ☐
4 I tend to get what I need from books and then
   move on. ☐
5 I can't understand the jargon. ☐

6 I can't see my way to applying all the ideas. ☐
7 The writers are unrealistic: it's not that easy to change
   working practices. ☐
8 Books can't really change anything. What counts is
   experience. ☐

 COMMENT

Now read through the comment for the points that you ticked.

1 Tone

Bear with us. This book is about positive action, not theory. And we want its style to reflect that. Our aim is to engage in dialogue with you, and to emphasize that we have used a generally informal style. We hope you will find this a refreshing change. If not, don't judge the content on the style alone. Think of the text as a trainer or seminar leader speaking, and focus on the content.

2 Time

If you feel you haven't the time to devote to this book, think again about the amount of time you spend tackling—or not tackling—people problems. The approach we suggest is intended to save you time, by taking a constructive, solution-focused approach that helps ensure problems don't recur. So the time you spend on this book should soon pay ample dividends in your day-to-day work.

3 Relevance

Unless you live cut off from all communications, you're unlikely to find this book irrelevant. All communication involves people, and so in turn throws up people problems. Likewise, the problem-solving approach we suggest can work as effectively by e-mail or telephone as face-to-face.

4 *You read and then move on*

That's fine by us. But we need to emphasize that you need to do more than dip into this book or half read it. You don't need to read every section, but you'll get the most out of the text if you take an in-depth approach to the material you do read. In particular we suggest you tackle the activities, which aim to help you think through issues yourself and apply them to your own situation.

5 *You can't understand the jargon*

If you find unexplained jargon in this book, please let us know and we'll score it out for the next printing. Our aim has been to make workplace problem-solving strategies accessible to everyone, without the need for any specialist knowledge.

6 *You can't see your way to applying all the ideas*

We don't expect you to transform your workplace into paradise overnight—or anytime. What we do suggest is a broad framework for problem solving within which you will be able to test out and build on our suggestions at whatever pace suits you best. And even if you apply just 10 per cent of our ideas, you should achieve substantial positive changes in your workplace.

7 *You think we're unrealistic*

Ingrained workplace practices are never easy to change. We recognize that. But this book isn't in the business of slick solutions. We are suggesting a carefully planned strategy for responding to people problems, built on a foundation of improved communication skills. It's a failure to address these issues that tends to prevent other improved practices taking root.

8 *What counts is experience*

You're right of course. Books alone can't change anything. But that is precisely why we have laid such stress on your own experience and judgement, by including activities and case studies in this text. Tackle these, and you'll be doing more than simply reading a book: you'll be actively reflecting on your own experience and developing real problem-solving skills.

Using this book actively

You can use this book in two quite different ways:

- As a short self-training programme to help you, the manager, develop problem-solving skills.
- As a reference tool, to help you identify ways of solving specific problems.

To enhance its value for each function we have included a number of specific aids, which we set out below.

 ACTIVITY

We suggest brief exercises you can work through to test out your skills and understanding. Try to set aside the time to do these. They are not an optional extra, but are integral to the book. Where appropriate, activities are followed by a comment section.

 COMMENT

This is not intended to be an 'answer'. By no means. It is simply our own response to the questions that have been posed. There are few absolute rights and wrongs in this field, though there are more, or less, appropriate strategies depending on the situation with which you are faced. So if you disagree with our comment, fine. And if you disagree very strongly or frequently we would like to know. Drop us a line, care of the publisher. We'll try to address your point in the next edition.

 CASE STUDY

We have included in this book over 30 case studies based on our experience as workplace problem-solvers. The names have of course been disguised, but every one is related to our own encounters with people problems and our developing understanding of how best to deal with these. We hope you find them a powerful way of increasing your grasp of problem situations and their solutions.

Effective learning is active learning

These aids are not an optional extra. We strongly recommend you to take advantage of them. Carl Rogers observed that little, if any, significant learning occurs as a result of simply being told. This is true for the problem-solving style we describe in this book and it is true for your own approach to the book itself. In order for the skills and ideas in this book to have a real impact on your effectiveness as a problem-solver, you need to take an active role in their development. Putting your mind to work on the case studies and activities in this book is a key to ensuring this.

Using the pages of this book as problem-solving tools

The aim of this book is to help you to deal with people problems at work. The principal way in which you can do this is through honing up your skills as a face-to-face problem-solver. Just as you are using this book to enhance your practice, you can also use it to help your colleagues develop their own skills as problem-solvers—providing they take the active approach we have recommended. So if you expect this book to be part of a private armoury of management techniques, bad news. You can use it in this way, but the approach we recommend is a more open one. If you are planning to try out the problem-solving approach with your colleagues or staff, *tell* them this. Bring them in on the act. Show them this book. Lend it them to take home. Because, as we have already emphasized, the ultimate agenda of anyone who deals with people problems is to empower others to deal with their own problems more effectively. Otherwise there's a danger that you will just encourage people to become dependent on you.

To emphasize this point we have designed this book in such a way that you can pass copies of individual pages to colleagues to assist in their own problem solving. We call this process *biblio-training*, from the Greek *biblios*, book. Pages that are designed for biblio-training in this way are highlighted by the following symbol:

The process dimension

As a problem-solving manager it is vital not only to practise skills but to be aware of the process you are involved in as you practise. As other writers on the subject have expressed it, it is vital to 'honestly examine and evaluate the assumptions and beliefs that dictate how we feel and what we do'. This means that at every point in the problem-solving process you need to be aware of:

● Not only *what* you are doing, or saying, but *why* you are doing or saying it.
● Not only *what* your colleague is doing or saying, but *why* they are doing or saying it.
● Not only what is being said or done *now*, but the *wider* pattern into which it fits.

Sometimes these wider issues will be evident; at other times they will be hidden away, and part of your skill as a problem-solving manager will be to help your colleague to become aware of them. You will also need to become aware of the issues yourself.

These points underpin the whole approach of this book, which takes us to the final part of this introductory chapter.

How this book is structured

The rest of this book is divided into seven chapters, as follows.

Chapter 1 enables you to examine your basic skills and knowledge about problem solving in the workplace, and outlines the understanding of human behaviour on which our approach is based. This section is not optional. You will get much more out of the book that follows if you first:

- Check out your own assumptions about what makes for effective problem solving.
- Review your current problem-solving skills—which you are almost certain to have. You then have the option either to work through the whole book systematically (which we recommend) or to begin by working through just those sections that are priorities for you.
- Ground your problem solving in a clear understanding of the way people tend to experience and react to workplace situations.

Chapter 2 looks at a range of essential listening and communication skills. You can use these in all your work with people, but particularly in dealing with problems. The section is self-contained, so that you can use it either as a brief self-training exercise in its own right, or as a quick reference guide, or—and this is its chief value—as preparation for the chapters that follow.

Chapter 3 introduces you to the 'ABCDE' framework for understanding and dealing with people problems. To get the most out of this chapter you will need to read through it systematically and tackle the activities you find there. Once you have got to grips with this framework you will find your problem-solving capability is greatly enhanced, particularly when you also bring into play the skills we explain in Chapters 2 and 4.

Chapter 4 follows on directly from Chapter 3. As we have hinted, it focuses on skills, this time on the more specialist range of skills you can use when working with the ABCDE framework. Like Chapter 2, you can use it both as a comprehensive, self-training exercise and as a reference guide to return to as and when you need it.

Chapter 5 draws together the four previous sections and shows you how to use your skills and understanding while following a systematic problem-solving agenda. This seven-stage agenda is indispensable. It guarantees that you follow through the task of problem solving as effectively as possible in the limited time available to you. It can be used in discussions of any length, from five minutes to one hour, and in one interview or over a series.

Chapter 6 offers a final selection of skills and strategies for use in association with your problem solving. The emphasis here is on ways of dealing with specific types of problem, and on deploying some more advanced problem-solving strategies—while building on the base set out in the previous chapters.

Finally, Chapter 7 looks at some wider organizational issues, in particular developing a wider problem-solving strategy. It is followed by a short appendix that lists organizations and self-help books that can further enhance your skill in dealing with people problems at work.

Summary

In this introduction we have looked at who this book is for and at how you can ensure that you make working through this book a priority task. We have explained that if you are to get the most out of this text you need to approach it as actively as possible, and we have explained how the book is structured. In Chapter 1 we will help you to review your expectations and skills and further clarify what is involved in dealing effectively with people problems.

Reviewing your expectations and skills

Aims

This short section will help you to:

- Explore your own assumptions about what makes for effective problem solving
- Review your current problem-solving skills
- Identify the skills you want to develop as a priority

We suggest you work systematically through the following activity and then compare notes with the comment at the end.

Exploring your assumptions

 ACTIVITY 1.1

Read each of the seven statements in Fig. Act. 1.1 (p. 2). Think carefully about

	Agree	Disagree
1 Dealing with people problems means being keen to help people.	☐	☐
2 Most people with problems need to be given clear solutions.	☐	☐
3 If you are going to deal with a problem effectively you need to have encountered something similar yourself.	☐	☐
4 Unless you can give advice you'll be no good at dealing with people problems.	☐	☐
5 You won't be able to deal with people problems if you get impatient with people.	☐	☐
6 Managers who don't encounter problems themselves are those best suited to helping others sort out theirs.	☐	☐
7 Staff who are in difficulties need practical advice first and foremost.	☐	☐

Fig. Act. 1.1 Exploring your assumptions

each one and tick the box in the right-hand column that most clearly matches your own response. Then compare your results with the comments that follow.

COMMENT

Let's take each of these points in turn.

1 Dealing with people problems means being keen to help people

There's certainly no harm in wanting to help other people. But you don't need to have a special urge to practise effectively as a problem-solver. What is more important is to care about the overall performance and quality of life in your workplace. In fact, we would go so far as to say that managers who have a really strong urge to help others may well be poor problem-solvers. The difficulty is that they will put their own need to help before the more pressing needs of the person they are helping.

2 Most people with problems need to be given clear solutions

Telling people what to do when they have problems is usually a very poor way of helping them. The chances are that they will take no notice. Or if they do, this will increase their dependence on you instead of helping them to be more independent.

3 If you are going to deal with a problem effectively you need to have encountered something similar yourself

If you have had experience of a similar difficulty this may increase your colleague's faith in your skill as a problem-solver, especially if they are looking to you for advice. However, every person and every situation is unique, and the solution that has worked for you may not work for them. And if you make too many comparisons with your own experience there is also a danger that you will become absorbed in recalling your own problem and not really take in what the other person is saying.

4 Unless you can give advice you'll be no good at dealing with people problems

This is just not true. There are times when it may be more appropriate to give advice; but the most important skill in your problem-solving toolkit is that of helping your colleagues to devise their own solutions. In that way your colleagues learn not only the right motions to go through for this particular case, but also the transferable skill of devising an effective problem-solving strategy.

5 You won't be able to deal with people problems if you get impatient with people

So who's perfect? In this book we recognize that everyone feels impatient, or angry, or frustrated at times. What is important is to understand why you feel that way and to learn not to let your feelings get in the way of dealing with the problem in hand.

6 Managers who don't encounter problems themselves are those best suited to helping others sort out theirs

If you agreed with this, which particular managers did you have in mind? Managers who think they have never had a problem are kidding themselves; and self-deception is definitely a handicap for anyone who wants to deal with people problems.

7 Staff who are in difficulties need practical advice first and foremost

Giving advice is only one aspect of dealing with people problems, and one that we deliberately downplay in this book. Staff in difficulties may well come to you looking for advice, but the chances are that in explaining their problem they will begin to recognize a possible solution, or realize that the advice they were seeking was not the best way of dealing with their problem.

Reviewing your skills

The sorts of skill with which this book deals are likely to figure in your own repertory already. In a sense there is nothing new here. However, in another sense, by working through this book you are starting out on something quite revolutionary. You are going to build on what you already do and learn to work:

● Systematically
● Reflectively
● Selectively

The last point is particularly important. We will be helping you to use skills with some discernment, and select just those that are most useful for the given situation. The following activity is intended to illustrate this.

 ACTIVITY 1.2

In Fig. Act. 1.2 (p. 6) we list a range of typical skills deployed by managers when tackling people problems. Rate each one on a scale from 1 (very often) to 5 (very rarely) in terms of:

● How frequently you use it now.
● How frequently you might hope to use it once you have finished reading this book.

Leave the third 'Priority' column blank for now.

 COMMENT

The skills with even numbers are all skills that this book will help you to develop. Those with odd numbers, on the other hand, are less likely to help you deal effectively with people problems, though some may apparently offer benefits in the short term.

		Now	Then	Priority
1	Giving advice	☐	☐	☐
2	Listening to what others are saying	☐	☐	☐
3	Asking penetrating questions	☐	☐	☐
4	Helping people clarify what they want	☐	☐	☐
5	Providing solutions to a problem	☐	☐	☐
6	Suggesting alternative ways of looking at a problem	☐	☐	☐
7	Keeping conversation going	☐	☐	☐
8	Helping people to make decisions	☐	☐	☐
9	Making people face up to their responsibilities	☐	☐	☐
10	Exploring the consequences of different solutions	☐	☐	☐
11	Pinpointing people's weaknesses	☐	☐	☐
12	Helping people to cope with difficult emotions	☐	☐	☐
13	Correcting people's misunderstandings	☐	☐	☐
14	Opening up a discussion	☐	☐	☐
15	Telling people how to tackle problems	☐	☐	☐

Fig. Act. 1.2 A range of typical managerial skills

ACTIVITY 1.3

So bearing in mind that it is the even numbered skills that are tackled by this book, go back to the chart and rate the skills in order of priority. Put a (1) next to the skill you rate as most important, a (2) next to the skill you rate as next in importance, and so on.

COMMENT

Now compare the skill numbers with the page numbers of this book.

Skill		Covered on pages
2	Listening to what others are saying	20–22
4	Helping people clarify what they want	101–114
6	Suggesting alternative ways of looking at a problem	71–94
8	Helping people to make decisions	129–134
10	Exploring the consequences of different solutions	125–128
12	Helping people to cope with difficult emotions	28–31
14	Opening up a discussion	12–18

You now have a choice of whether to focus just on those skills that you see as current priorities or to work through the book as it is written. There is no single correct approach, though we do recommend that if you dip into specific sections you skim through the rest. This will help you to gain an understanding of the overall strategy for problem solving, as well as the specific skills involved.

What dealing with people problems is not

It should now be clear that our overall aim is to help you build up a range of skills that:

● Enable others to deal with their problem effectively.
● Build up others' skills in avoiding, or anticipating, or dealing with problems in the future.

Our aim is *not* to build up your skills in:

● Solving other people's problems for them.
● Encouraging your staff to depend on you for solutions.

In fact, we hope that this book will help you actively to avoid the second type of skill.

Let's summarize by listing some of the pitfalls that the problem-solving approach is designed to help you avoid. Here are some typical approaches to people with problems, and why you need to be wary of using them.

A summary: pitfalls to avoid

Do something . . . anything

You may feel that dealing with a people problem means taking action on their behalf. Unless you actually do something you won't really be helping them.

Think again

Taking action on someone else's behalf is only one way of tackling a problem, and is unlikely to be the first of your strategies. At the least you need to postpone action until your colleague has had the chance to fully articulate the problem confronting them.

Help them to look on the bright side

You may feel a strong urge to help the other person accentuate the positive, count their blessings.

Think again

This approach may sometimes be appropriate, but again you will need to use it with great caution. Trying to cheer up someone who is feeling depressed can result in them feeling even worse, adding a burden of guilt at feeling so negative. Our approach is not about positive thinking—it's about constructive, realistic thinking.

Sort the problem out for them on the spot

Perhaps you know just how they feel, and you can see exactly what the solution is.

Think again

No one, repeat no one, knows exactly how anyone feels. Maybe we can hazard an informed guess, but then only when we have given the other person a reasonable chance at articulating their problem. And explaining their problem to you will almost certainly involve explaining it to themselves as well, in which case they—not you—are likely to be at least half-way towards a solution. Bear in mind too, that the most effective solutions are self-suggested; advice on its own may be only a partial way of dealing with a people problem.

Take their mind off the problem by telling them about yourself

You feel it will help to show the other person that they are not alone. You can share your problems with them, too.

Think again

This may momentarily distract, but it has nothing to do with dealing effectively with people problems. The only way to do this is to give the other person free rein to explain their situation, their thoughts, their feelings. Anything that blocks this, at least at the start of a problem-solving encounter, is likely to be counter-productive.

Pass on some useful tips

You have read a book that you have personally found very helpful. You want to tell the other person that it's bound to assist them with their problem.

Think again

Telling people rarely has positive results. If you doubt this, think of what you have learnt—the really significant things—and how you learnt them. The chances are that you learnt some significant facts by being told, but the rest will have been a matter of first-hand experience and reflection.

You are now ready to look in more depth at some of the skills involved in dealing with people problems at work.

References

Dryden, W. and Gordon, J. (1993) *Peak Performance: Becoming More Effective at Work*, Mercury Business Books, Didcot.

Ellis, A. and DiMattia, D. (1991) *Rational Effectiveness Training: A New Method of Facilitating Management and Labor Relations,* Institute for Rational/Emotive Therapy, New York.

Kirby, P. and DiMattia, D. (1991) *A Rational Approach to Rational Living*, Wilshire Books, North Hollywood, CA.

Palmer, S. (1994) 'Stress management and counselling: a problem solving approach', *Stress News*, vol. 5, no. 3, pp. 2-3.

CHAPTER **2**

Essential listening and communication skills for the problem-solving manager

Introduction

In this chapter we explain a range of key listening and communication skills that you can deploy in your work as a manager. We will be returning to these throughout the book: they are the essential underpinning for the more advanced skills that we explore in later sections. But they are also valuable in themselves, for use at any time, whether or not you are consciously engaged in 'problem-solving': in fact, by practising these skills you are likely to forestall problems that might otherwise occur. So you can use this section in all or any of the following ways:

● Work through it now as a self-contained skill-enhancement exercise
● Work through it now as a preamble to the more advanced skills that follow
● Use it as a quick-reference or refresher whenever you are presented with people problems in the workplace.

Effective communication

Communicating effectively involves developing your skills in:

● Responding
● Listening

Let's review each of these in turn.

Responding

Here we want to focus particularly on responses that help to clarify a problem. There are two main parameters here:

● Open questions and closed questions
● Inviting responses and discerning responses

Let's take each of these in turn.

Open or closed?

All questions we ask of other people fall somewhere between the open and the closed.

The more closed a question, the nearer it gets to inviting a response of either 'yes' or 'no'. Questions that invite a 'maybe' or 'perhaps' are still more or less closed. They offer an interpretation, or an answer, or a solution and simply ask the person questioned to sign up to it; or not. Here are some examples.

1 Did you mean to come in late?
2 You're upset aren't you?
3 Have you been doing this for a long time?
4 Is it hard to imagine yourself succeeding?

This approach presents several barriers to effective problem solving. It:

● Presents you as an interrogator.

- Forecloses any wider discussion.
- Tends to force a particular interpretation onto the person being questioned.
- Conveys the message that you are in charge of the exchange, increasing your colleague's long-term dependence on you as a problem-solver.
- Sounds as if you are figuring out or verifying your own hypothesis.

In contrast to a closed question, an open question is *open* to any response: it invites the person questioned to find their own words, which may or may not be in line with what you as a questioner anticipate.

 ACTIVITY 2.1

If you are unfamiliar with the distinction between open and closed, try putting questions 1–4 in the list into a more open form. Then compare notes with the comment below.

 COMMENT

Here is just one possible reframing:

1   What was the reason for coming in late?
2   How are you feeling now?
3   How long have you been doing this?
4   How easy is it to imagine yourself succeeding?

Less closed but still restrictive

Even without inviting a simple 'yes' or 'no' we can still, inadvertently, constrain the other person's response.

ACTIVITY 2.2

The following questions could pose problems. Why do you think this is? Ponder this point before continuing—unless, of course, you feel really confident that you're able to go for openness.

1   When did you stop sleeping well?
2   How are you feeling . . . OK?
3   What organization are you calling from?
4   Why do you punish yourself like that?

 ## COMMENT

1   The problem with this response is that it is loaded with assumptions—that the other person has indeed stopped sleeping well, or that they understand what you mean by 'well', or that they can put their finger on the time when their sleep problems began.
2   This is a typical example of a question with a smuggled-in answer. The questioner seems to be asking the other person to respond positively, and is making it difficult for them to respond with something like 'I'm feeling lousy actually'.
3   This is a question that the switchboard operators of a training organization habitually asked until someone pointed out the problem they created when freelance trainers rang. For anyone who was not a member of an organization the question was unanswerable, and sometimes left them feeling wrong-footed before they even began their enquiry.
4   'Punish' is a loaded term, and may not be appropriate to the way the person feels about their actions. Again, the question is restrictive because it is loaded with certain—in this case quite emotive—assumptions.

The distinction between open and closed questions is, of course, only a relative one. For example, if in a closed question you pose all the possible alternatives, you are in effect asking an open question. Nor are we suggesting that you consciously appraise every question before you pose it. It's more important to get into the habit of approaching people problems with an open frame of mind. Don't get hung up on 'getting it right'. Otherwise you will distract yourself riffling through a directory of correct responses when your real task is to attend fully to the person you are with.

'Why' questions

Here it's worth highlighting another type of question that hovers on the boundary between open and closed: the 'Why' question.

Think about a question starting 'Why . . . ?'. Much depends on your manner, of course, but the danger is that you may be interpreted as asking your colleague to explain themselves. Alternatively, you may come across as trying to figure out your own hypothesis.

Inviting responses and discerning responses

The other parameter we identified was that of inviting responses and discerning responses. Let's look at each in turn.

Inviting responses

An inviting response is designed to invite some initial discussion of the issue. At this stage it is vital not to make any assumptions about the issues involved. Jumping to conclusions may create blocks in your relationship with your colleague that are hard to dismantle. Take the following exchange, for example.

 ## CASE STUDY 2.1

Josh   I need to talk to you about my case-load.

Saville   Yes, we're all finding things a strain this year. I can help you with last month's but you'll need to stick with September's.

Josh   It's not so much the amount . . .

Saville Right, there are a lot of tough problems, and I can see they've been on your mind.

Josh I can manage OK with most of them, it's just that . . .

Saville Yes. Moana said that Systems Support complained about traffic flow. I'll sort that out myself.

Josh It's none of that.

Saville OK. What is it?

 ## ACTIVITY 2.3

Think for a moment about this exchange.

What do you think is wrong with it?

How might Saville have dealt more effectively with this people problem?

If you like, jot down your response before comparing notes with the comment that follows.

 ## COMMENT

Saville takes a sympathetic approach to Josh, but does not follow one of the first and most important guidelines when approaching people problems. He has immediately assumed what the problem is. Here's how the exchange might have developed had he been more aware of stage 1 of the problem-solving approach.

Josh I need to talk to you about my case-load

Saville OK. I can see it's on your mind. Tell me a bit about the problem.

Josh Well I've been dealing with complaints about traffic flow; and the other morning we had a mother asking about her son's M70 papers, which I had to trace.

Saville   And you're finding this sort of work a problem?

Josh   I am, yes.

Saville   Do you want to say a bit more about what the problem is?

Josh   Well, yes. Frankly I'm bored out of my mind by this routine work. Can't I get my teeth into something more challenging?

A very different outcome to the earlier one. And note that being prepared to invite a response means being prepared for surprises!

The key inviting response here is 'Tell me a bit about the problem.' There are plenty of other ways of inviting discussion. We list these in Table 2.1. For heaven's sake don't try to memorize these: dealing with people problems isn't a question of wheeling out stock responses at the appropriate stage. Instead, browse through the list and try to gain a sense of what the responses have in common. We have left a space at the end of the table for you to add your own ideas, both now and as your problem-solving skills develop.

Table 2.1   Inviting responses

Responses that help to invite discussion include:
- Do you want to tell me about the problem?
- You appear to be having difficulty achieving your targets recently. Would you like to discuss this with me?
- I've noticed you've been rather irritable recently. Do you want to talk about it?
- You've been working really long hours for the past month. Perhaps there's a problem we should look at.
- How are things going?

Your own suggestions:

Discerning responses

Once opened up, a problem-focused discussion may take any number of courses. Your colleague may be reluctant to say more; or you may find you have unlocked a torrent of words, revealing a confused tangle of issues and incidents. However, in all cases your key aim here is to help the other person to be as specific as possible.

There is a typical example of a discerning response in the case study. Think about it now. It was Saville's final response: 'Do you want to say a bit more about what the problem is?' But there are plenty of other possibilities, as shown in Table 2.2; once again we have left space for you to add your own ideas.

Table 2.2 Discerning responses

Responses that help the reluctant colleague to clarify issues include:
- Do you want to tell me/say more about the problem?
- Could you explain that in more detail?
- What is it about … that concerns you?

Your own suggestions:

Responses that help a verbose person to clarify issues include:
- You've explained what's happened over some weeks. Perhaps you could describe the most recent incident?
- You've mentioned quite a few different issues. What do you think about making a list of the main points?
- I can see what you're getting at in general. Could you now give me one or two examples?

Your own suggestions:

Being concrete

In the early stages of a problem-solving discussion you will frequently be presented with very general statements. These need to be made more specific and concrete if progress is to be made towards a solution. However, try to resist any urge in yourself to criticize a colleague for speaking in a general way; they may find it difficult to talk about what is on their mind and their first, tentative steps towards the problem may need to be in the form of generalizations. Aim to gently persuade them to make a more concrete statement, using the type of response that we have identified here.

Table 2.3   Being concrete

General statement	Concrete counterpart
1(a) They are all talking about me.	1(b) Gemma and Steve are talking behind my back.
2(a) Losing my job means 'kaput'	2(b) Clark, my neighbour, had a breakdown when he was fired.
3(a) Gays just shouldn't be allowed in this firm.	3(b) I think Adam's style of dressing gives the firm a bad name.
4(a) No one gets listened to.	4(b) I've been complaining about the cloakroom for months: it's still just as bad.

Table 2.3 suggests a small range of general statements, together with the concrete counterparts which you could aim to elicit by sensitive questioning. Responses that could elicit some of the information in these concrete counterparts might be as follows:

1   Could you tell me a bit about who these people are?
2   When you say 'kaput' could you tell me what you mean?
3   Is there any particular person you have in mind when you say that?
4   I'd find it helpful if you could give me an example of someone not being heard.

Frequently, statements made in response to this sort of question can be further concretized. However, these further details may well emerge naturally in the course of your discussion and you need to strike a careful balance between working with generalizations and probing too intensively.

Listening

In practice, listening and responding are different aspects of a single, integrated skill. So some of the points we make here are really about responding, but in a way that reassures the other person they are being heard and helps them maintain the flow of their own account. Listening skills are also a way of enabling your colleague to open up without feeling in any way pressured or manipulated.

First let's look at three specific types of 'listening response'.

Minimal encouragers
A minimal encourager is the name that has been given to the wide range of short utterances all of us use to indicate that we are paying attention. We all have our own characteristic set of such encouragers, and none is more or less appropriate than any other. However, in any problem-solving communication it is useful to remind yourself of the value of responding in this way. Typical words include:

- Aha
- Uh-huh
- Umm
- Ye-es
- Right

But just as important as the word itself is the tone and manner in which you say it, and the point at which you utter it—perhaps accompanying the encourager with a gentle nod. This may be particularly appropriate when something difficult or embarrassing is being disclosed, as a way of helping your colleague to feel accepted, rather than judged.

CASE STUDY 2.2

Richard	Then Clare complained that I'd been eyeing her up
Viv	Uh-uh [*minimal encourager*]
Richard	She said I was in despatch too often for her liking…
Viv	[*Nodding*] mm
Richard	. . . and that other people were, er … remarking on it.

Verbal bubbles

In dealing with people problems it can be helpful to use verbal bubbles, particularly in situations where you want to gently guide your colleague back to what seems to be the key issue. The following case study provides a typical example. See if you can identify it.

 ## CASE STUDY 2.3

Richard	Of course, it wasn't a problem in my own office. I don't think anyone there has an inkling of what Clare has said.
Viv:	So you feel more relaxed when you're at your own desk?
Richard	Oh yes. In fact, I managed to get a new office chair from Tyndalls, you know, the sort with swivel arms . . .
Viv	. . . which you can rest on when you're not typing.
Richard	That's it. They say it's a good way of avoiding repetitive strain injury.
Viv	Right. [*Pauses*] I'm just wondering to myself, though, whether this might be taking us away from the issue of Clare.
Richard	It's still on my mind, yes. And the truth is, I do quite fancy her.

The bubble is in Viv's final response—where you'll see that it is also accompanied by a minimal encourager. Viv is gently drawing Richard back to the problem agenda with which he started, and helping him to focus on it, even though this may be more of a challenge for him than talking about the office furniture!

Companion responses

A companion response is a listening response because it stays with what the other person is saying, without intruding on their line of thought. Companions go along with the flow of discussion—in contrast to bubbles, which may constructively cut across it.

 ## CASE STUDY 2.4

Viv   You find Clare attractive.

Richard   And that's part of the problem. Because I *have* been looking at her, but not in the way she seems to think.

Viv   She seems to you to be putting the wrong interpretation on things?

Richard   Yes, I find it really upsetting. I feel so . . . so misunderstood.

Working with silence

At the outset, your discussion may well be marked by silence. For example, suppose a colleague has come to see you about a 'problem' they are experiencing in their department. They seem very uneasy. Your dialogue goes as follows:

You   OK, feel free to tell me whatever's on your mind; we've got twenty minutes or so and I've had calls diverted.

Colleague It's hard to know where to begin. Things have been getting difficult lately.

              [*Your colleague falls silent.*]

ACTIVITY 2.4

Which of the following is closest to your own likely response? (This isn't a test of your understanding; put down the response that reflects your actual practice rather than what you believe you should do.)

1 Wait until they start talking again, no matter how long that is?
2 Wait for a few moments and then ask them: 'Do you want to say more?'
3 Wait for a few moments and then ask them: 'I wonder if you really want to talk with me now?'
4 Wait for a few moments and then prompt them: 'Things have been getting difficult?'
5 Wait for two or three minutes and then ask them 'How are you feeling right now?'
6 Wait for a few moments and then ask them: 'Why have you fallen silent?'

 COMMENT

Our suggestion would be, in descending order of preference:

4   2   5   1   3   6

If you have ever experienced counselling, as opposed to problem solving, you may be surprised that we have placed (5) and (1) lower than (4) and (2) . But we want to emphasize that a problem-solver is not the same as a counsellor. Within the limitations of your work role there is unlikely to be time to wait in a totally open-ended way for whatever your colleague wishes to disclose (1); and focusing on the immediate process between yourself and your colleague (5), though a powerful tool in counselling, may raise issues that it is difficult to deal with in the confines of a work setting. We discuss this point further on page 31, under the heading 'Immediacy'.

On the other hand we would have reservations about responding on the lines of either (3) or (6). Both have an interrogative tone that is likely to put your colleague on the defensive, particularly if they feel unsure of themselves, or wound up in some way.

Indeed, it could have continued in a similar vein:

Alan   [*Nodding*]   Things aren't going right?

Geoff   No. [*Silence. Looks down. Clears his throat. Long pause.*] Things at home are difficult. [*Further pause. He rubs his eyes with his hand.*] I'm not sleeping. Can't concentrate. [*Further long pause. Looks uneasy.*]

One of the most important basic principles of dealing with people problems is that silence is OK. Indeed, silence may communicate as much as speech. Accepting your colleague's silence can:

● Help emphasize that in this situation, the agenda is under their control.
● Give you both time to reflect on the situation.
● Develop trust.

If possible, wait for your colleague to break the silence; or if you sense hostility or unease, intervene with a simple enquiry, for example:

Alan   Would it help to say a bit more about what things are difficult at home?

Of course, you will need to be aware of the silence you can afford, given the time available; but allowing for this, resist the temptation to intervene just because your colleague is not speaking.

So use silence sensitively, and try to give it a place without treating it either as a shortcoming or as an opportunity for playing at therapy—which is definitely not your role as a workplace problem-solver. Most of us tend to avoid silence, and the chances are that, as a busy manager aware of a whole host of tasks that need performing, you fall into this category. Make a point, then, of going along with pauses. Give your interview time to breathe!

When discussion gets stuck

Particularly when your colleague is exploring difficult concerns, there may be points at which your discussion comes to a halt. You can deploy a number of techniques to help minimize this:

- Reflection on a word or phrase
- Paraphrasing what has been said
- Summarising what has been said

Let's look at each of these in more detail.

Reflection

Reflection on a word or phrase means just that: mirroring what your colleague has said. By doing this you:

- Help to reassure them that they have your full attention.
- Can communicate your understanding from their perspective or frame of reference.
- Can enable them to maintain a clear focus on their concerns.
- Help to build up trust.

Here is an example of what we mean. We have put the reflective response in bold in each case.

 CASE STUDY 2.5

Alpana has come for a chat with her manager Abdul. Her concern is a recent incident in which she felt she was being subject to sexual harassment. Here are some snapshots of part of the conversation.

Alpana   So its been several days since I've been in his office and I feel
. . . well [*struggling*] … inhibited.

Abdul [*Nodding*] **Inhibited.**

Alpana Yes. I feel that I can't just act in a normal way. I try to avoid the department as far as possible.

Alpana I met him last week in the supermarket and he seemed to be looking at me in an odd sort of way.

Abdul **An odd sort of way?**

Alpana As if I'd offended him. I don't know what to think, really I don't.

Alpana I mean, it's bad enough with all the pressure at home, all piling up like that.

Abdul **Piling up.**

Alpana Piling up?

Abdul You just said that.

Alpana Yes. So why did you repeat it?

We have included the last snapshot to show that there is always a danger of overdoing this and other reflective skills. Like all the other problem-solving skills in this book, you need to deploy them with great sensitivity, and beware of taking a mechanical approach. The skills we discuss are not techniques for manipulating your colleague: they are ways in which you can increase their capacity to solve their own problems.

Paraphrasing

Paraphrasing is in some ways similar to reflection of a word or phrase. The difference is that you are translating and summarizing your colleague's words in a way that is helpful to them, enabling them to clarify their concerns. Here are two further snapshots from the discussion between Alpana and Abdul. Again, we have put the paraphrasing responses in **bold**.

Alpana I find that if I'm just sitting in the office he sometimes walks past, and goes just a bit closer to my desk than he needs to. I know he's aware how it's upsetting me. He's trying to wind me up even more, and the worst thing is, he's succeeding.

Abdul **So it seems that he knows how you feel and he's doing his best to make you feel worse?**

Alpana Right. And I want all this to stop. I can't take much more…

And later:

Alpana Something bad happened in my last job: really bad I mean. It began a bit like this and then one day this guy cornered me. I ended up leaving. And now I find myself thinking: Well, here we go again.

Abdul **You're worried that what's happening now may be the start of the same sort of trouble that hurt you before.**

Alpana That's right. I just couldn't stand another experience like that one. I think if it happens I'll just fall apart.

Notice that in these two examples, Abdul isn't offering any sort of special insight: he is simply expressing in different words (and more concisely—though this isn't essential) what Alpana has already said. Alpana's response suggests that this is helpful. It helps reassure her that Abdul has heard and understood what she is saying, and also helps her to pause briefly and take stock.

Using metaphors

You may sometimes find it helpful to paraphrase by using metaphors. These can be a very effective way of re-presenting a person's problem in a way that enables them to more fully grasp its true nature and extent. Take Abdul's final response to Alpana, for example. He could have said:

Abdul It sounds a bit like you feel you're finding yourself on a sort of roller coaster which you'd rather not be on.

Alternatively, Abdul could have invited Alpana herself to suggest a metaphor:

Abdul I'm wondering if there's any sort of picture that sums up how you're feeling at the moment?

Alpana [*After a pause*] Right now I see, like, a sort of roller-coaster with me just being pushed into a car ready to shoot up and over the top; terrifying, really.

Always be tentative in your use of metaphors, though. What strikes you forcibly may not be at all the right match for your colleague—hence the value of inviting them to paint their own picture.

Paraphrasing feelings

So far we have looked at interactions that emphasize the content of your interview. For example, when you offer a paraphrase you are helping your colleague to gain a clearer picture of their situation. However, when it begins to look as if there may be an emotional block to effective problem solving you will find it useful to at least tentatively offer your own perception of what your colleague is feeling. In this sense you are paraphrasing or reflecting their feelings. This can help them to acknowledge their emotions and recognize that you are aware of them.

Look for expressions of feeling in any of the following ways:

Verbal expressions

Listen out for the use of verbal expressions that convey feelings. Words such as 'frustrated', 'bored', 'irritated', 'shocked'.

Non-verbal expressions

Look out for non-verbal expressions that can provide useful clues to feelings. Here are some typical examples:

- Speed of speech
- Loudness of voice
- Tone of voice
- Bodily tension or relaxation (e.g. in the hands or in the jaw)
- Blushing
- Turning away from, or making, eye contact

When you notice feelings in this way, try to bring them to the attention of your colleague, but be sure to do so in a tentative way, as we have already suggested for paraphrasing. Try, too, to acknowledge the strength of your colleagues feeling—bearing in mind that overstressing may be as offputting as underestimating!

Here are two examples of exchanges in which feelings are being reflected.

Example 1

Colleague   So I get home in the evening and just sit in front of the TV; Moira puts the children to bed and sometimes I hardly seem to notice that they're there at all.

Manager   You sound as if you're really regretting the toll that work takes on you and the lack of energy you have for your family.

Example 2

Colleague   When we won the tender it was great. I'd always wanted to visit Japan and now I had the prospect of three or four trips in the space of a few months.

Manager   You'd become really excited at the prospect, hadn't you?

These examples emphasize that in order to reflect feelings in a constructive way you need to:

● Put a name to them
● Take a tentative approach (e.g. 'It sounds . . . ', 'You seem . . .')

You may also sometimes find it helpful to offer a tentative context. For instance, in example 2 the manager might, in the light of more information from his colleague, have said: 'You seem to get really excited whenever a project is about to take off'.

Summarizing
Summarizing is a further way in which you can assist your colleague to get to grips with the nature of their problem. In offering a summary you are both

paraphrasing and drawing together what your colleague has said.

Use summaries:

● To recapitulate.
● Following discussions that have been long and complex, to check that you have understood what your colleague is saying.
● When you feel that everything has been said and that your interview is over.
● At the end of a time-limited interview, as a résumé before discussing the next step.

Here's how Abdul summarized his conversation with Alpana after she had finished explaining her problem to him.

Alpana   So there it is. I feel one hundred per cent sick and tired of the whole situation.

Abdul   Right. I can see that you're upset. You feel that this person has been making suggestive comments to you, and has made matters worse by approaching you in the office and outside, and that this is a situation that might get a lot worse—to the point of you wanting to find a job elsewhere.

And here's a summary from a quite different situation. Ellen feels that she has been passed over for promotion in favour of a younger but less experienced woman. Ken is her manager.

Ellen   It's made me feel like a nobody. Me. The things I've done for this department. Well, sod the lot of you I say.

Ken   Let's get this clear. You feel that you are really well qualified for the job—more than Kerry—and that it has gone to her just because she's younger; and you feel insulted and passed over by what has happened.

Again, notice that these really are just summaries. No interpretation is being offered. At this stage in the interview it is generally not appropriate to do more than simply help your colleague to articulate the issue that is on their mind. Dealing with people problems requires a light touch initially. Even if you feel drawn to interpreting the problem or suggesting a possible solution, be aware that your view can only be tentative.

Finally, bear in mind the usefulness of summaries in helping your colleague keep to the point. Rambling is endemic to most conversations, but your joint task is to make the most of the inevitably limited time at your disposal.

Immediacy

Reflecting feelings can have a very powerful effect on your interview if you focus on the feelings that your colleague is immediately experiencing. However, approach this form of interaction with extreme care, since immediacy may unlock emotions which are difficult to cope with in a work setting and which will leave your colleague and yourself feeling uneasy and embarrassed. Here are two contrasting examples of the use of immediacy.

Example 1

Colleague   And so when Gill comes into the office with that stupid grin on her face I start to get worked up inside. I can see her now, standing there.

Manager   You're really feeling that anger now, aren't you?

Colleague   Of course I'm bloody 'feeling that anger'. Do I look as if I'm bloody meditating? Don't come at me with your 'interpersonal' bullshit. You're as bad as she is.

Example 2

Colleague   I don't know quite where to start. Erm . . . it's difficult . . . with people in the office. Erm . . .

Manager   You're a bit nervous about talking to me like this, right?

Colleague   [*Relaxing*] Well yes, yes I am, it seems so trivial. But I do need to get it off my chest.

In the first example the intervention serves only to exacerbate feelings in an unhelpful way; in the second it relieves them. There are no hard and fast rules here, and you will need to develop your own sensitivity over time. But if in doubt the best strategy is probably restraint on your part.

Expressing your own feelings

You will encounter many occasions when you can usefully express your own feelings. In fact, sharing your feelings can have a very powerful effect on the dialogue. Try to get into the habit of monitoring your own feelings as they arise, and be prepared to share them. This can have some useful effects.

- It can indicate to your colleague that it is acceptable to speak about feelings.
- It can build up a climate of trust between you.
- It can provide helpful information to your colleague.

Here are some typical examples of disclosures of this sort.

1   I feel a bit worn by the number of criticisms you're making of other staff. Maybe I'm not alone in this.

2   When you are avoiding issues like that I feel irritated. I wonder if other people in your office might react in a similar way?

3   When I hear you say that I feel quite sad. Perhaps you're feeling upset by the situation yourself?

You need to handle these disclosures with great tact. Throughout the discussion you need to communicate acceptance rather than personal criticism. Handled differently, each of the three examples above could lead your colleague to pull up a defensive drawbridge rather than feel encouraged to disclose more about their problem.

ACTIVITY 2.5

Think for a moment about each of the examples.

How might they have been handled less constructively?

You may find it helpful to jot down your ideas before reading the comment that follows.

 COMMENT

The disclosures could have been expressed less constructively as follows:

1 I'm fed up with the way you're constantly criticizing others and so are other staff.
2 These evasions are really irritating—not just to me but to people in your office.
3 That's really saddening. You must be terribly upset.

Let's think about how the first set of responses differs from the second.

● The first set describes feelings while the second set describes a situation. The first three statements are one person's response to another person. As such, they are open to make no claim to be absolutely valid. However, they do provide useful information to the colleague, which can help them in the ways we have explained.
● The first set are tentative while the second set claims to be definitive. The first three statements implicitly give your colleague permission to challenge, qualify, or reject them if they wish to.

If in doubt…

As we have emphasized, disclosing feelings can have a very powerful effect at this—and indeed at any—stage in the problem-solving process. You will probably find it best to work in this way only if you feel fully confident, and to take fairly tentative steps in this direction. So if in doubt, keep quiet.

Acknowledging feelings

But even if you opt for silence, make a point of acknowledging feelings. Be aware of your own reaction. For example, during an initial discussion the speaker in (1) might have thought:

> I'm feeling irritated. I wonder why that is? I'd better relax or my frown might appear judgmental.

This sort of reflection still has a lot of value. By becoming aware of your own feelings you can:

- Gain insight into one of the factors critical to the success of your discussion.
- (In some instances) remove a potential barrier to effective listening.

We'd like to end this chapter by explaining the last point in a little more detail.

Discounting feelings

We have explained that any disclosure of feelings to your colleague needs to be tentative. There should always be a possibility of discounting feelings. One reason for this is that your feelings may come from either of two sources. They may arise from:

- an accurate appraisal of the situation
- blocks in yourself.

 CASE STUDY 2.6

Kieran had asked to meet Gerry over lunch to discuss a personal problem.

Gerry was aware that Kieran had recently taken several days leave at short notice to care for his wife while she recovered from a hysterectomy. As lunch progressed Kieran explained that he wanted to take up the firm's offer of a new teleworking arrangement for two days a week. This would enable him to help with the care of his two school-age children while his wife convalesced. Gerry felt unaccountably resentful of Kieran's request. But rather than letting this influence his reaction, he set his feelings on one side, making a mental note to consider them that evening.

When he did run over his reaction to Kieran he recalled an incident some years ago when his own boss had turned down a request for shorter hours while he cared for his mother during her final illness. The pain of this refusal had influenced his reaction to Kieran's request which he was able to recognize as entirely reasonable.

Genuine or not?

This case study emphasizes a further important point. In any encounter with a colleague, try to be as genuine as possible. But also consider the context in which you are working. You are not a counsellor. Your overall aim as a manager is to get jobs done. It may not always be appropriate to say exactly what you think, and while integrity may require us to speak the truth, it does oblige us to voice our feelings at every opportunity.

For example, it would have been quite inappropriate for Gerry to express his resentment towards Kieran as it would not have helped the problem-solving process. Instead, he was able to acknowledge the feeling, but then to respectfully lay it on one side until he had the chance to reflect on it further. Similarly, if you feel the person you are in dialogue with is a worthless little shit, it is unlikely to help the process to express this, however justified you feel your opinion to be.

On the other hand, if you are problem solving with a workplace bully it may be very helpful to give information about your own feelings—which might involve frustration, anger, or even fear. This information, presented in an unconfrontational way, might come as a revelation to a staff member who justifies bullying as harmless banter and has never fully comprehended the feelings it occasions in others.

Summary

In this chapter we have looked at a range of key communication and listening skills for use in any dialogue with your staff. These skills are valuable in themselves, but they really come into their own as part of a wider-ranging problem-solving process. In the next chapter we introduce a framework for understanding problems at work and then, in Chapter 4, explain the process itself.

References

Brammer, L. M. (1988) *The Helping Relationship: Processes and Skills,* 4th edn, Prentice Hall, Englewood Cliffs, NJ.

Culley, S. (1991) *Integrative Counselling Skills,* Sage, London.

Dainow, S. and Bailey, C. (1988) *Developing Skills with People: Training for Person to Person Client Contact,* Wiley, Chichester.

Ivey, A. E., Ivey, M. B. and Simek-Downing, L. (1987) *Counselling and Psychotherapy: Integrating Skills, Theory and Practice,* 2nd edn, Prentice Hall, Englewood Cliffs, NJ.

Mearns, D. and Thorne, B. (1988) *Person-centred Counselling in Action,* Sage, London.

Nelson-Jones, R. (1989) *Practical Counselling and Helping Skills,* 2nd edn, Cassell, London.

Palmer, S. and Dryden, W. (1995) *Counselling for Stress Problems,* Sage, London.

Reddy, M. (1987) *The Manager's Guide to Counselling at Work,* Methuen, London.

Truax, C. B. and Carkhuff, R. R. (1967) *Toward Effective Counselling and Psychotherapy,* Aldine, Chicago.

CHAPTER 3

A framework for problem solving

Aims

This chapter will enable you to:

- Get to grips with two key frameworks for dealing with people problems.
- Recognize the critical role of beliefs in problem solving.
- Help staff and colleagues tackle the emotional consequences of unreasonable beliefs.
- Challenge staff and colleagues to develop more healthy emotions in response to a problem situation.

The ABC framework

We have already looked at the important distinction between perception and actuality. This distinction underpins the approach to human behaviour on which much of this book is based. The approach was developed by a well-known psychologist, Dr Albert Ellis, who called it the ABC model, and later expanded into the emotional problem-solving framework of ABCDE. Here we'll use the term 'framework' instead of 'model', which more accurately describes the function of ABC in dealing with people problems.

The ABC framework is based on research carried out by psychologists into the root causes of emotional disturbance.

A stands for the *activating* event
B stands for *belief system*
C stands for the *consequence*

This is shown in Fig. 3.1.

Activating event ⟶ Beliefs ⟶ Consequence

Fig. 3.1   ABC framework

We'll explain this framework in more detail shortly. The point we need to stress first is that the framework suggests that distress is not the direct result of the problems we encounter. Rather, it often arises from the misguided assumptions we make about them. The best way to tackle emotional upset is therefore to identify these assumptions and systematically root them out by applying clear logic.

The ABC framework in action

We are going to illustrate the value of the ABC framework right away, with the help of an activity. This activity is probably one of the most important exercises in this book and we recommend that you set aside about five minutes to undertake it. Whatever happens, please do not overlook it as it helps to explain how we largely contribute to our own problems in the workplace.

 ACTIVITY 3.1

Just imagine arriving late for an important meeting. We'll give you a few moments to picture this happening. We call 'arriving late' the activating event, or 'A' for short.

Now imagine you hold the following beliefs, known as 'B', about turning up late:

> I must not arrive late, but if I do it would be awful, it would prove I am a useless manager and I could not stand it.

How would you feel? Would you feel:

	Tick
Angry?	☐
Anxious?	☐
Depressed?	☐
Guilty?	☐
Ashamed?	☐

 ## COMMENT

How you feel is known as 'C': the consequences. Depending upon how you felt, 'C' may also involve a behavioural component such as withdrawal, shaking your fists, or running around like a headless chicken.

The ABC can be easily represented as follows:

A Arriving late for an important meeting
B I must not arrive late, but if I do it would be awful; it would prove that I am a useless manager and I could not stand it.
C Emotion: anxiety and depression (or whatever your emotion is)
Behaviour: running around like a headless chicken, not being able to concentrate.

 ## ACTIVITY 3.2

Now let's imagine that you held different beliefs that were similar but were not inflexible, absolutist and rigid. Once again, imagine that you are arriving late for an important meeting, but the only difference is that this time you are telling yourself something like:

> I strongly prefer not to arrive late, but if I do it would be bad but certainly not the end of the world and awful. It may indicate that I have some management skills deficits but certainly not that I am a completely useless manager. I've been late before and even though it was unpleasant I am living proof that I can stand it.

How would you feel this time? Would you feel:

	Tick
Annoyed?	☐
Concerned?	☐
Sad?	☐
Remorseful?	☐
Regretful?	☐

 COMMENT

If you truly believed the new beliefs, would you feel as disturbed as you did in the earlier example? We doubt it. Once again this can be represented diagrammatically as follows.

A Arriving late for an important meeting

B I strongly prefer not to arrive late for an important meeting, but if I do it will be bad but certainly not the end of the world and awful. It may indicate that I have some management skills deficits but certainly not that I'm a completely useless manager. I've been late before and even though it was unpleasant, I am living proof that I can stand it.

C Emotion: concern
   Behaviour: after arriving late, focus on making up for lost time and not wasting valuable seconds blaming others or myself.

Notice how by taking a different attitude to arriving late—holding more helpful beliefs—you can remain problem focused. In addition, notice how some emotions do not necessarily distract a person from the job in hand, whereas others are more self-defeating and prevent a person from achieving their goals. Although many emotions are negative some are more negative and unhelpful than others. Table 3.1 illustrates the main unhealthy negative and healthy negative emotions.

Table 3.1   Healthy and unhealthy negative emotions

Unhealthy negative emotions	Healthy negative emotions
Damning anger	Non-damning anger (or annoyance)
Anxiety	Concern
Depression	Sadness
Guilt	Remorse
Shame/embarrassment	Regret
Hurt	Disappointment
Morbid jealousy	Non-morbid jealousy

As in the earlier example, the healthy negative emotions involve flexible and realistic thinking, whereas unhealthy, negative emotions involve evaluative, dogmatic, rigid, and unrealistic thinking. Unhealthy negative emotions invariably involve 'musts', 'shoulds', 'oughts', 'got tos', and 'have tos', which can lead to evaluative derivatives such as:

I am worthless/useless because. . .
It's awful that . . .
I can't stand it that . . .

This is in contrast to healthy, negative emotions which involve preferences, wishes, desires, and wants.

Table 3.2, adapted from *Counselling for Stress Problems* (Palmer and Dryden, 1995) not only summarizes some of the main unhealthy and healthy negative emotions but also links these to the typical situations in which these emotions tend to arise. We suggest you use this as a quick reference only: in the first instance it is usually better to invite your colleague to propose an emotion that will enable them to cope with their situation more effectively and constructively. If they cannot find an alternative then you could discuss an alternative from the table.

Table 3.2 Healthy and unhealthy negative emotions

Perceived situation	Emotion	Healthy/ Unhealthy
Threat or danger	Anxiety	U
	Concern	H
Loss; failure	Depression	U
	Sadness	H
Breaking of moral code: self	Guilt	U
	Remorse	H
Breaking of moral code: other	Damning anger	U
	Annoyance	H
Display of personal weakness	Shame	U
	Regret	H
Betrayal of self by other	Hurt	U
	Disappointment	H
Threat to exclusive relationship	Morbid jealousy	U
	Non-morbid jealousy	H

Irrational beliefs and unhealthy emotions

We hope we have now clearly demonstrated the way in which unhealthy emotions are underpinned by irrational beliefs. These beliefs may be about:

● The situation in which a person finds themselves.
● Their emotional response to that situation.

In other words, even if a person's beliefs about an external circumstance are well-founded, their response may be constrained by their beliefs about themselves. In this case, problem solving will involve focusing more directly on the emotion.

Emotional problem solving in action

Let's now see how the ideas we have outlined might translate into action.

 CASE STUDY 3.1

Viv was a manager in an electrical components firm. She came to her boss concerned at the difficult negotiations she was having to conduct with the trade union, who were challenging the need for what the firm saw as a necessary restructuring. Viv's boss had recently been on a short course in problem solving and suggested that the first step should be for Viv to take an assertive approach and set out the firm's position to the union rep. Several days later Viv took sick leave, and after a fortnight handed in her notice, having found a less well-paid job with another firm. It turned out that Viv had never arranged to meet with the rep. She was so anxious about creating a scene that she had procrastinated and avoided discussion.

 COMMENT

In the case we have just described, assisting Viv would involve first helping her to look at the emotional side of the issue and find ways of managing her anxiety, such as challenging her thinking errors. Only then would she be in a position to focus on how to handle the reaction of the rep. In other words, an approach focusing only on what action Viv should take would almost certainly come unstuck. Instead the priority is to home in on the emotion.

For example, Viv's boss could encourage her to imagine meeting up with the union rep, and then consider what might be hindering her from doing so. A good question her boss might ask would be 'Just imagine that you are going to speak to your rep. How do you feel about doing this?' If Viv were to reply 'Very anxious' the anxiety would be the emotional block that she would need to deal with before the task was carried out.

A more advanced illustration

In Viv's case the emotional block to problem solving is directly related to the matter in hand. However, many of the people problems you encounter may be less clear cut. Here is a more advanced illustration of the ABC framework, bearing in mind all we have said about emotional problem solving.

 CASE STUDY 3.2

Mavis had applied for promotion to another department in the marketing company where she worked. Having applied for the job with high hopes, she had been rejected after the first interview. She subsequently became deeply depressed and became increasingly behind in her work.

The *activating event* in this case is Mavis's rejection

The *consequence* is Mavis's feelings and reaction.

The key to understanding the framework is to realize that, contrary to common sense, A was not the direct cause of C. To pinpoint the cause we need to look at a further factor: the *belief system,* which in this case is represented by Mavis's beliefs about the job she had set her heart on and her ideas about herself in relation to the job.

Let's see how the ABC framework might be applied to help Mavis tackle her problem. Her depression was the result of irrational beliefs at B such as:

- *I can't stand* being turned down.
- Not being accepted for the job is *a disaster.*
- With my qualifications I really *should* have been accepted. The fact that I haven't been shows that either the interviewer didn't like me or that I'm *no good.*

These beliefs are unhelpful and irrational because they prevent Mavis from reaching her goals of keeping up with her work without becoming stressed and depressed.

ACTIVITY 3.3

From what we have now discussed you should be in a position to spot why these beliefs are irrational. We suggest you pause now to consider this before continuing. (But it's up to you . . . read on if you're pressed for time.)

And as a further check on your understanding, see if you can identify a further set of *rational beliefs*.

COMMENT

Right. Now compare notes.

I can't bear being turned down.

It might be helpful to ask Mavis what she really means. Does she think she will literally come apart at the seams? Mavis thinks she can't stand being rejected, and because she thinks in this way she will feel in this way too. But of course, as long as she is alive and breathing she can in fact stand anything. In fact, she had been standing being rejected for over four weeks.

Or perhaps when Mavis says she can't stand it means that she'll never be happy again. But short of facing execution, Mavis probably has as much chance of finding happiness in the future as anyone else.

Not being accepted for the job is a disaster.

We need to ask Mavis where the evidence is for this. The chances are that the disaster is a result of thinking that the situation is disastrous. And what does 'disastrous' really mean? It's certainly very inconvenient for Mavis not to be accepted but by using a term like disastrous she seems to be demanding that life must absolutely not be inconvenient in this way. This hardly seems to be a reasonable demand. And by making it, Mavis seems almost to be inviting emotional disturbance.

I really* should *have been accepted.

If Mavis really should have been accepted then she would have been. The universe would be structured in that way. Thinking otherwise is likely to lead to damning anger and frustration.

. . . Either the interviewer didn't like me or I'm no good.

It may have been the case that the interviewer didn't like Mavis. But neither he nor she is particularly good or bad. They are both fallible human beings.

We also asked you to try to identify a set of more helpful, rational beliefs that Mavis might hold in relation to her rejection. She might have believed, quite reasonably that:

- Rejection leads to fewer chances of advancing her career or less interesting work.
- Without the new job she would have less money.
- Work would be less interesting in the future.

In the light of these rational beliefs it would be appropriate for Mavis to feel annoyed and sad; but these feelings are very different from the damning anger and depression resulting from the irrational beliefs that we have identified above.

We wonder how far you anticipated these comments. If you did, or if you were able to make similar ones, then you are already on the way to understanding the foundations of the problem-solving approach. However, it is one thing to agree in principle that misconceptions similar to those of Mavis are at the root of the majority of people problems. But it's quite another to put into practice a problem-solving approach based on this insight. That can be your aim as you work throughout the rest of this book.

Now let's see what would have happened if Grant, Mavis's manager had noticed that she was underperforming but had not appreciated the emotional roots of her problem. The dialogue might just have gone like this.

Grant   Right Mavis, take a seat.

Mavis   [*Looking downcast*] Thanks.

Grant   I want to talk to you about schedules. You've been getting behind with orders recently.

Mavis: Well yes, I just don't seem to be have the energy I used to have. I'll try to push ahead next week.

Grant   OK, that sounds sensible. How about setting yourself some targets. Why don't you make a note of the number of packages you plan to clear by the end of each day, and then check your progress at lunch and before you leave?

Mavis   [*Unenthusiastically*] Fine. I'll get you a list tomorrow…

Grant   … and we can check through it together and agree that you'll try to meet the targets.

Good practical problem-solving material. The difficulty here is that Grant has failed entirely to recognize that Mavis is depressed, and for reasons only indirectly related to her immediate work situation. Or possibly he has noticed it but feels powerless to help her. However, unless he acknowledges these feelings there is likely to be little prospect of Mavis meeting her targets. In fact, the problem is likely to get worse rather than better.

Once feelings are admitted into the equation there is a greater possibility of lasting change occurring. Grant could help Mavis recognize that the roots of her depression lie in her thoughts about the interview situation rather than the situation itself. Freed of the emotional burden of these mistaken assumptions, Mavis could then tap the energy necessary to achieve her targets. Obviously, if she was very depressed then Grant could suggest that she could visit a doctor or counsellor to help her deal with the way she felt.

A recap

Note—again—that it is the beliefs (B) a person holds about a specific situation or activating event (A) that largely contribute to the consequences (C) and *not* the event itself. This makes our task of dealing with people problems easier. When the situation or stress scenario cannot be changed, we can help our colleague or member of staff look at the situation differently and thereby become less stressed. In many cases this helps the person to remain problem-focused and more likely to resolve or manage the problem. Our view—and this is backed up by a widely recognized bank of academic research—is that personal belief systems are the key to a wide range of people problems and their solution. These irrational, or self-defeating, systems result in problems. These can be systematically examined and replaced by rational, or self-helping, ones. In this process the person gains the insight to control, rather than be controlled by events. They no longer see themselves as a victim.

So to recap, the ABC framework introduces an important element between the *Activating event* and the feelings that occur as a *Consequence* of the personal *Belief systems*. These are critical in influencing our ability to cope with events. When people problems occur they are frequently the result of irrational beliefs. By helping your staff to take a rational view of their own, frequently unvoiced, assumptions you can give them the tools to tackle their own problems in a really effective way.

Over to you

Now that we have fully described the ABC framework, let's conclude with two activities in which you can practise applying it for yourself. The first is based on two case studies.

ACTIVITY 3.4

See if you can identify the three elements in each of the situations that we outline below. You will need to use your imagination for the second.

CASE STUDY 3.3

Sue

Sue has presented a report to her boss, Alan, mid-morning, after working hard on it until late the previous evening and going into work early to prepare a final draft. Alan had emphasized to her that this was an important report, and was needed by midday at the latest. At midday she bumped into Alan in the corridor. 'Have you read the report yet?' 'No, not yet, I'll take a look at it over lunch.' At lunchtime Sue noticed Alan in the canteen chatting to colleagues while thumbing through the report. She appeared in Alan's office after lunch with an irate look on her face. 'I'm really angry. I was up till late last night finishing that report', she protested 'and you've hardly touched it. I thought my work was more important to you than that. You should take my work seriously.'

 CASE STUDY 3.4

Ben and Gary

Gary seems to be continually in conflict with Ben. Both work in the maintenance department of a large machine-tool manufacturer. You suggest each in turn visits you to discuss the situation. Ben explains: 'Gary's always looking down his nose at me. He makes me feel as if I'm being checked up on all the time'. Gary explains: 'I feel I need to be on my guard against Ben. He's shifty and unreliable. It makes him really hard to work with.'

 COMMENT

You could have said something like the following:

Sue

- *Activating event:* Alan's review of the report in the canteen.
- *Belief about the event:* Sue believed that Alan's behaviour was a sign that he didn't value her work—'I thought my work was more important to you than that.'
- *Consequence:* Sue became angry about Alan's behaviour as she also believed (at B) that he *should* have taken her work seriously.

Ben and Gary

- *Activating event:* Ben was slightly built and dark, and spoke quickly and rather indistinctly with a strong regional accent. Gary was slower and methodical with an upper-class accent.
- *Belief about the event:* Gary believed that people who looked and sounded like Ben were likely to be less reliable—and staff should be reliable. Ben believed that people who spoke and behaved like Gary were likely to be very judgemental—and people should not be judgemental.
- *Consequence:* Gary and Ben clashed and were angry with each other not because of any genuine differences in approaches to their work but because of their ingrained beliefs about one another, based on personal stereotypes and also their 'shouldy' demands about other people's behaviour, i.e. how other people *should* or *should not* behave.

Make a point of reflection on problems you encounter over the coming weeks in these terms. See if you can identify the three elements – particularly the beliefs which are responsible for the reaction. Your aim as a problem-solver should be for this way of viewing problems to become second nature, and the foundation for finding appropriate solutions.

The second of our two concluding activities is a more open-ended one, in which you will need to put yourself in the place of a manager facing a typical— perhaps *the* typical—difficult situation.

 ACTIVITY 3.5

Suppose you are a manager who has to break news of job-loss to a member of staff. What might their reaction be in terms of the ABC framework? See if you can map out the possible A, B, and C. You may, of course, suggest more than one point for the B and C. Spend up to ten minutes on this activity before comparing notes with our suggestions below.

COMMENT

Here is how you could have mapped out your employee's reaction to losing their job.

A = activating event	Receiving notice of losing the job
B = beliefs	I didn't perform as well as I should have
	I absolutely should have a job
	I am a total failure and am worthless because I have lost my job
	It's awful that I've lost my job
	I can't stand losing my job
C = consequence	Depression
	Future avoidance of work associates
	Difficulties with sleeping
	Can't be bothered to send CV to new potential employer.

The ABCDE framework

As you get to grips with the basic ABC framework you will be able to use it as a powerful tool for tackling a variety of people problems. In order to do this you need to add two further components:

D *disputing* of the unhelpful belief
E identifying *effective behaviours.*

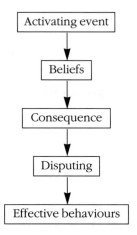

Fig. 3.2   ABCDE framework

Figure 3.2 is an extended version of Fig. 3.1, showing how the further stages fit in.

Disputing the belief

Although we have used the word 'dispute' here, we are not suggesting that you approach colleagues with all guns blazing. Throughout this book we emphasize the importance of taking a tentative approach to any hunches of your own, and inviting, rather than demanding, a response from your colleague.

 ACTIVITY 3.6

Return to the two case studies, of Gary and Ben, and of Sue. Suppose you are the manager of Gary and Ben, or are in Alan's place. How might you gently dispute or challenge the beliefs they hold in each instance?

Make a note of your response before continuing. Don't be tempted just to read on: remember that learning depends on engaging actively with the topic.

COMMENT

Alan could have suggested:

> Does the fact that I was talking to friends necessarily mean that the report is of little value to me? Maybe the issues I was discussing with my colleagues were even more important than your valuable report?

Gary and Ben's manager might have suggested (to either of them):

> It would be useful if you could give me a specific example of when you became angry and clashed with Gary/Ben.

The effort involved in getting to grips with constructive disputing is well worth while, and you will have ample opportunity to do this as you progress through this book.

Identifying effective behaviours

This is the final component of the problem-solving framework. You have now achieved clarity about the problem. Together you have identified the activating event, the belief about it, and the problematic consequence. You have disputed the belief, and you are now in a position to help your colleague identify an effective way of proceeding, based on a more accurate perception of the situation.

Here is how the two situations we have been considering were resolved.

With Alan's help, and discussion of the ABC framework, Sue realized that she had put just one construction on the situation. In fact, the two colleagues Alan was chatting to were offering some vital information about a competitor's plans. Alan was torn between listening to them and reviewing the report.

Together Sue and Alan agreed that it would be helpful if in future Sue made a point of verifying her perception of situations before reacting to them. This was Sue's 'effective behaviour'. In fact, learning about the ABC framework made all the difference to Sue: far from feeling attacked by Alan's problem-solving approach she saw him as offering her an important item of new information and support, which made all the difference to her approach to relationships at work. Alan also showed Sue how her 'shouldy' demands exacerbated her anger.

The problem affecting Gary and Ben was resolved in a different way. Neither of them were able to give any convincing, specific examples of behaviour that adequately expressed why they became stressed about each other. Their manager then briefly introduced them to the ABCDE framework and asked them to think whether this might shed any light on what the real issue was. In fact, Ben and then Gary realized that they tended to see each other as stereotypes, and recognized that this had no foundation in actuality. The tensions didn't disappear completely, but they were able to work in a more constructive manner without any further serious disputes. The manager also illustrated how their 'shouldy' demands helped to raise their stress levels.

By the way: share your skills!

The Gary and Ben case also underlines how valuable it can be to share your understanding of the problem-solving process. You may find this difficult. You may feel we are suggesting that you give away power. If so, ask yourself what your goals are at work. If your main goal is to perform as well as possible in your job role, then you won't achieve this by making others dependent on your problem-solving skills. On the contrary, you are more likely to perform effectively if you give others the tools to deal with their own problems. On the other hand, your goal may be to become your organization's agony uncle or aunt. In that case, you probably need to apply for a different job. And you certainly don't need to continue with this book.

Thoughts and feelings

For the rest of this chapter we want to home in on how people experience problems, and why they experience them as they do, looking in more detail at the role of thoughts. This provides essential underpinning knowledge as you dispute unreasonable beliefs and identify effective behaviours.

So let's take a closer look at B: beliefs. The first point we need to make is that it's rarely possible to find out about the role of beliefs in a people problem simply by asking someone to explain the situation as they see it. There are three reasons for this:

● What a person says they believe may not be what they actually believe.
● The beliefs that really exacerbate a problem are often deep-seated ones, of which the person is entirely unaware.
● Beliefs may act as a filter through which the world is experienced. We may be no more aware of these than we are of a pair of spectacles when we are wearing them.

We'll take these points in turn.

Espoused belief versus lived belief

When trying to establish what a person believes it is useful to have in mind the difference between *espoused beliefs* and *lived beliefs*.

If we use simple questions to try to find out what makes a person tick, we are likely first to elicit espoused beliefs. For example, we might ask:

● Is free and open communication important to you?
● Should managers listen to their staff?
● Should women have the same opportunities at work as men?

Well yes, of course. The chance are we do espouse these beliefs. But they may differ considerably from the beliefs we demonstrate by our actions—our lived beliefs.

Lived beliefs are those we demonstrate by our behaviour. They may be unacknowledged, and may be directly opposed to our espoused beliefs. This is not to say that we are hypocrites: the contradiction between our espoused belief and belief-in-practice may be:

- Hidden from us, simply because we have never reflected on the links between our beliefs and our behaviour.
- Reasoned away by special pleading, which allows us to maintain both beliefs simultaneously. For example, we may think that there are particular circumstances that allow us to transgress an otherwise absolute rule.

 ACTIVITY 3.7

Here are three further espoused beliefs. For each one, see if you can suggest :

- A countering, lived belief.
- An example of special pleading that would enable us to justify both espousing the belief and practising otherwise.

Ethical investment is the only acceptable form of investment.

Families need to spend more time together.

Team working is vital to me.

 COMMENT

Our own suggestions are given in Table 3.3. Yours will be different, but check that they are on the same general lines.

Beliefs and problem solving

Exploring beliefs is a vital aspect of dealing with people problems. Sometimes it may be sufficient simply to review espoused beliefs. These need not necessarily be contradicted by lived beliefs, and to assume such a contradiction might

Table 3.3 Comment on espoused beliefs

Espoused belief	Belief-in-practice	Special pleading
Ethical investment is the only acceptable form of investment.	I invest wherever I can be reasonably sure of a very good return.	My job is very insecure and I need to save up for the children's school fees.
Families need to spend more time together.	I spend Sundays with the children but the rest of the week is for work and sport.	I have a high-powered job that demands my time, and gives the children other sorts of benefit.
Team working is vital to me.	I prefer to work on my own; that way I can be sure of being in control.	None of my colleagues are the sort of people who could gel into a proper team.

harm the trust that needs to exist between yourself and your colleague. However, there will be occasions when espoused beliefs seem to be at odds with a person's behaviour. When this occurs you will need to be prepared to challenge your colleague's behaviour and beliefs, drawing attention to this apparent contradiction. In this way they can work towards a deeper understanding of what they really believe, and become more aware of why they react to situations as they do.

We will explore the skill of challenging later in this book, in Chapter 4. Now we want to look further at lived beliefs, and note the tendency they have to intervene between activating event and consequence. In particular, we want to review the way in which they act as templates through which we experience the world.

Tackling templates

Template is a term usually reserved for things, but it can also be applied to people. Here we are using 'template' to describe a habitual way of looking at the world. Someone who looks at the world through rose-tinted spectacles might just as well be described as using a rose-tinted template.

In dealing with any people problems we need to be alert to the way in which these templates are used—how far they can contribute to the problem or its solution.

Here's an example of how the issue of templates might come up in practice. In Case Study 3.5, Ros is talking to Ken, who has been falling behind in his work. Ken seems to Ros to be a perfectionist. He seems to have low self-esteem, and is becoming increasingly anxious about the quality of his work and his inability to meet deadlines.

 CASE STUDY 3.5

When Ros first asked Ken whether he thought he was appreciated, generally, at work he nodded emphatically. 'Yes, I think I am', he explained, and added 'I know my work's crucial to profitability, and the department's turned in some good results lately.'

 ACTIVITY 3.8

● Is there anything in Ken's response that might suggest a possible underlying problem?
● What in Ken's behaviour might confirm this?
● If you were Ros how might you respond to Ken?

 COMMENT

What is a little odd about Ken's response is that he doesn't really back up his belief that he is appreciated. All he suggests is why he thinks he *ought* to be appreciated. So perhaps his espoused belief is at odds with an underlying, template, belief.

Let's just suppose that Ken really sees himself as undervalued – at work, and perhaps generally. We might expect him to show this in his behaviour by:

- A tendency to seek frequent reassurance that his work is valued.
- Going well beyond what his job role requires in an attempt to win praise.

Your response might be on the lines of:

It's interesting to hear you say you feel appreciated. Sometimes you appear to me as someone who needs quite a lot of reassurance that your work is valued. I wonder how that squares with your own feelings.'

Note that Ken could experience this as quite a powerful challenge. As we explain later, you will need to develop a skill in posing these challenges in a firm but tentative way.

Let's see how Ros's chat with Ken in fact developed.

In response to Ros's questioning, Ken admitted—to himself, as well as to Ros —that he tended to see himself as undervalued. He saw the world through a template: no one really appreciates me. This led him to go to great lengths to win his colleagues' approval, which in turn led to a loss of esteem. So Ken's habitual response to situations at work was part of a vicious circle. Fortunately Ros had been able to use her problem-solving skills to help Ken become aware of this unconscious template and view the situation in a different way.

This doesn't mean that Ros needed to be a counsellor to work effectively with Ken. As we have emphasized, this book is about solving problems, not offering therapy. But it does mean that when we are in similar position to Ros we may need to explore some of the lived beliefs of our colleagues, and help them understand how far they form templates for the whole of their experience.

We have looked at the possible contradictions between espoused and lived beliefs, and at the part the latter play in influencing our reactions to situations. For the final part of this section we want to look at another aspect of template-type beliefs, which may be entirely, or partly, outside our direct awareness.

Tackling distorted thinking

So far we have looked at fairly simple beliefs, which may lie anywhere on a continuum from entirely justified to completely erroneous. However, some beliefs can be more accurately thought of as habitual ways of thinking. When these ways of thinking become distorted they can function in just the same way as simpler beliefs, and skew our experience of what other people say and do. One of the key problem-solving skills is then to unskew the thoughts, and help eliminate the problem consequences (C in the ABC framework).

Let's look at one of the most common forms of distorted thinking, and at the problems to which it gives rise.

Thinking errors

Psychologists have identified 12 thinking errors that hinder problem-solving. Here are some of the commonest ones.

● All or nothing thinking

We see things in absolute, black-and-white terms, without any shades of grey.

Examples

If I fail at any important task, as I must not, I'm a total failure and completely unlovable.

A job isn't worth doing unless I do it extremely well.

I hate my boss; he's utterly useless. I've got no choice but to quit my job.

● Jumping to conclusions

We draw the worst possible conclusion from events or a situation—typically the conclusion that reflects most poorly on ourselves.

Examples

Since they have seen me fail, they will view me as utterly incompetent.

Because I made a mistake people will see me as appallingly careless and won't give me any other work.

She didn't respond when I greeted her, so she must think I'm not worth getting to know.

● Fortune telling

We assume that because things are not so good now they will continue this way, or worsen, in the future.

Examples

They are laughing at me for failing and therefore they'll despise me forever.

I feel down this morning; this must be the start of a bad week.

The copier's broken again; it'll take an age to mend and then my work will be totally disrupted.

● Discounting the positive

We give credence to criticism, but tell ourselves that any positive feedback has a hidden, negative agenda, or is insincere.

Examples

When my boss compliments me she's just being kind and avoiding mention of all my mistakes.

I did well in my appraisal, but that was just because I was lucky and they didn't ask any awkward questions.

He said it was a good report but that was just because he didn't have time to read it properly.

● Minimizing

We make excuses for our successes or strengths, and condemn ourselves for what we see as shortcomings or weaknesses.

Examples

My successes in sales were just freaks, but the deals I failed to win were my fault and were inexcusable.

When I'm ahead of schedule it's because the work is undemanding; when I'm behind I'm being incompetent.

● Emotional reasoning

We assume that the way things feel to be is the way they really are.

Examples

I feel like a total failure for performing so badly and because I feel so strongly that proves that I really am a failure.

She made me angry so she must have treated me badly.

I don't feel like ringing suppliers today, so I'll do it when the time seems right.

● Personalizing

We blame ourselves for something for which we are not really responsible.

Examples

Because my secretary has given her notice it's all my fault.

If I'd reminded him earlier he wouldn't have forgotten his appointment.

The company's performing badly. I should have pulled my weight more.

● Phoneyism

We interpret any apparent disparity between our self-image and the way others see us as implying that we are phoney.

Examples

When I don't do as well as I ought and they still give me more work, I am a real phoney and I'll soon fall on my face and show them how useless I really am.

He said he could trust me. Any day now I'll do something that shows how unreliable I really am.

● Perfectionism

We condemn ourselves for not fully achieving an impossible goal.

Examples

I know I did quite a good presentation, but it should have been perfect, and so I'm incompetent.

I got the job finished fairly promptly, but it should have been completed early to show how committed I am to the firm.

We were only a few per cent out in our forecast, but a person with my experience should be absolutely accurate every time.

● Mind reading

Reasoning from actions to thoughts, with negative consequences for yourself.

Examples

She must think I'm totally useless for not meeting the deadline.

He smiled at me; that must mean he's about to break some bad news.

She's looking upset; it must be something I've said.

● Labelling

Globally rating yourself—or others—as opposed to rating specific behaviour.

Examples

As I failed my exam, this proves that I am a complete failure.

He arrived late—he's totally incompetent.

You've bust the keyboard; how is it that you're so utterly useless?

ACTIVITY 3.9

As a way of getting to grips with thinking errors, we suggest you rate yourself against each type, using the grid in Table 3.4. Use the following scale:

1 I think like this very frequently.
2 I think like this quite frequently.
3 I think like this occasionally.
4 I never think like this.

To make this exercise easier, think back to the last time you became stressed about a specific event or situation.

We will be looking at ways of tackling thinking errors and other forms of distorted thinking in the next chapter. Our aim at this point has been to give you a general view of the ways in which beliefs can negatively affect our reaction to people and situations. And by the same token, an effective way of ensuring a more positive reaction is to revise these beliefs.

But it would be a mistake to see the solution of people problems as simply a matter of ironing out misunderstandings. Sometimes the consequence of our beliefs—of the template through which we interpret the world—involves such powerful emotions that we need to tackle these before we can return to work on revising the beliefs themselves.

Our assumption has been that a major cause of people problems in the workplace is not any specific situation as such, but the way in which the situation is perceived. Correct the distorted view and we go a long way towards dealing with the problem.

An advanced technique

Now you have almost finished Chapter 3 we would like to focus on one more problem assessment method that we have found useful on hundreds of

Table 3.4 Thinking errors self-audit

Belief	Your example	Your rating
All or nothing thinking		
Jumping to conclusions		
Fortune telling		
Discounting the positive		
Alls and nevers		
Minimizing		
Emotional reasoning		
Personalizing		
Phoneyism		
Perfectionism		
Mind reading		
Labelling		

occasions. If you are keen to read Chapter 4 by all means skip this part. However, we would recommend that you return to it later.

Inference chaining

When a person is stressed about a situation, often it is not really the event itself that the person is most stressed about. On many occasions it is some *aspect* of the situation or event.

We would like to share with you a powerful tool to elicit the underlying problem that a member of your staff may really be upset about. This advanced technique is called inference chaining. It involves chaining together a set of inferences or interconnecting issues about a particular problem to discover the underlying fear. Incidentally, an inference is an interpretation which goes beyond observable reality, but gives meaning to it. It may be accurate or inaccurate.

Here is how Kaye, the manager of a sales team, mapped the anxiety of Ron, who was finding it hard to cold-call important customers. While Ron responds to her questions, she writes his answers on either a whiteboard or a sheet of paper.

Kaye So you're finding you put off calls to important clients, and as you know, there have been a number of complaints.

Ron Right.

Kaye We spoke about this problem last week. It seems that you're still avoiding making the calls even though you agreed to make them.

Ron I just seem incapable of making them.

Kaye Hmm. We need to sort this out. I've got an idea how we can get to the root cause of the problem. Do you want to give it a go?

Ron OK. I've got nothing to lose.

Kaye And perhaps all to gain!
[*Kaye starts to inference chain.*]

	Just imagine for the moment that you're about to telephone an important client. [*Kaye pauses for a few seconds to allow sufficient time for Ron to imagine ringing an important customer.*] How do you feel?
Ron	Anxious.
Kaye	What is anxiety-provoking in your mind about actually speaking to an important customer?
Ron	Well, I suppose I'm afraid of bad news?
Kaye	Bad news?
Ron	Yeah—maybe they'll say they've cancelled their order.
Kaye	Well let's suppose that they have cancelled the order. Why do you get anxious about that?
Ron	I get worried that I'll get no more commission and that would look bad.
Kaye	And if that was true?
Ron	I might lose my job and never get another good job again!
Kaye	[*Kaye now maps out the inference chain for Ron and refers to the whiteboard.*] OK Ron. I want to recap. Which of these are you most anxious about:

    speaking to a customer
    getting bad news
    being told that they have cancelled an order
    getting no more commission
    looking bad
    losing your job
    never getting a good job again?

Ron	It's not so much the bad news. And frankly, it's unlikely that I'll lose my job. I reckon that I really get stressed about looking bad in front of my colleagues.

Note that in this example the true activating event or 'A' (from the ABC model) was not making telephone calls to his customers but 'looking bad in front of my colleagues'. Now this becomes the gateway into finding his self-defeating or irrational thinking. Note carefully Kaye's response.

Kaye   Now really imagine that your colleagues are thinking badly of you.

Ron   No trouble. I remember the last time it happened.

Kaye   What are you telling yourself?

Ron   I should always do well. They think I'm useless. And if that's true it would be really awful!

Kaye   As long as you believe that you 'should always do well' and if you don't they would think you're 'useless' and it would be 'really awful', how will you feel?

[Kaye is hoping to show Ron the disadvantages of holding these self-defeating beliefs and thereby encouraging him to challenge them later in the session.]

Ron   Anxious.

Kaye   Would it be helpful to look at your thinking and attempt to deal with your anxiety?

Ron   I'll give it a go.

This dialogue took no more than five minutes, yet in that time Ron discovered three components of the ABC framework:

A Looking bad in front of colleagues
B I should always do well; I'm useless; It would be awful
C Anxious; avoids telephoning customers

We usually find it useful to complete the ABCDE problem-solving form (see p. 132) when we reach this stage and then help the employee to dispute their unhelpful thinking. We deal with this in Chapter 4. Bear in mind, however, that the ABCDE framework may sometimes need supplementing by practical problem-solving skills.

Summary

This brings us to the end of Chapter 3. We hope you now have a framework for understanding some key aspects of human behaviour, and the key role played by our beliefs in the way we experience the world. We also hope you have a clear sense of the role of emotions in people problems.

In Chapter 4 we look at some of the additional skills you will need in order to make the most of the ABCDE framework. Then in Chapter 5 we will move on to look at seven key stages for dealing effectively with people problems.

References

Beck, A. T. (1976) *Cognitive Therapy and the Emotional Disorders,* New American Library, New York.

Burns, D. D. (1989) *The Feeling Good Handbook*, William Morrow, New York.

Ellis, A. (1972) *Executive Leadership: A Rational Approach,* Institute for Rational Emotive Therapy, New York.

Ellis, A. (1996) *Better, Deeper, and More Enduring Brief Therapy: The Rational Emotive Behaviour Approach,* Brunner/Mazel, New York.

Ellis, A. and Harper, R. A. (1975) *A New Guide to Rational Living,* Wilshire Books, North Hollywood, CA.

Ellis, A. and Blum, M. L. (1967) 'Rational training: a new method of facilitating labor relations', *Psychological Reports,* vol. 20, pp. 1267–1284.

Lange, A. and Grieger, R. (1993) 'Integrating RET into management consulting and training', *Journal of Rational-Emotive and Cognitive-Behavior Therapy,* vol. 11, no. 2, pp. 65-76.

Neenan, M. (1993) 'Using RET in the workplace', *The Rational-Emotive Therapist,* vol. 1, no. 1, pp. 23–26.

Palmer, S. and Dryden, W. (1995) *Counselling for Stress Problems*, Sage, London.

CHAPTER 4

Essential thinking skills for the problem-solving manager

Some basic logical tools

First let's look in what may seem an unexpected direction: to classical logic. This field has been guarded by academia for too long. Traditionally reserved for classicists, mathematicians, and philosophers, it is a rich source of powerful thinking tools that can greatly enhance the performance of any work-based problem-solver.

So let's look at four key logical tools you can call upon for this, and some of the logical pitfalls from which thinking errors arise. These tools divide into two categories. First we cover those that you need to discern illogical thinking; then we look at those you need in order to challenge this thinking.

Detecting illogical thinking

He would *say that* . . .

Most of us have encountered people problems in which the truth of an assertion is at stake:

- An unfavourable sales statistic has been quoted, the salesperson involved doubts its accuracy.
- A member of staff claims harassment, the person she is accusing denies responsibility.
- A doctor has diagnosed alcoholism, the person affected denies they have a problem.

In these and many other situations the doubt tends often to focus not on the facts themselves but on the person making the assertion, and their possible ulterior motives in doing so. Unless this is detected at an early stage it can effectively subvert the problem-focused interview. For example, here's how the first case above might present itself in practice. Paul is a manager in an electronics firm. He is meeting Kevin, whose performance seems to be suffering as a result of a mix of domestic and work pressures. Kevin is reluctant to admit any drop in performance:

Paul   Gerry tells me that your sales last week slipped well below twenty thousand—and that wasn't an optimistic target, was it?

Kevin   Well, I guess anything above twenty thousand would be reasonable . . . but wait a minute, Gerry has never been happy with my promotion. I mean, he would say my sales were down, wouldn't he? You've seen how he treats me at conferences . . .

Paul   So you feel Gerry resents your position?

At this point the discussion is in danger of going off the rails. Kevin is questioning the facts by questioning the motives of the person who has offered them. But Gerry's feelings towards Kevin have no bearing whatsoever on the accuracy of the figures. 'He (or she) *would* say that . . .' is never a helpful response in relation to a factual assertion, and can cloud discussion of the real issue. In this case the effect is to draw attention away from the issue of Kevin's underperformance onto the tension between himself and Gerry. This may be a significant issue but it is not on the agenda at this point.

Keep a close watch for the 'He would say that…' tendency in dealing with people problems. If necessary, make a mental note of the need to return to the personal issue at a later point, but don't allow it to distract you and your colleague from establishing a foundation of mutually agreed facts.

You might find it useful at this point to return to the remaining two issues on the list above and consider how the distortion we have identified here might impact on them.

No true manager

At an early stage in the problem-solving discussion it is often valuable to help move the discussion away from generalizations and to focus on the concrete. We have already mentioned this on pp. 19–20, but it is worth emphasizing the logical move involved at this point. The 'no true manager . . .' way of thinking (we'll explain the significance of the label shortly) is relevant wherever you sense that your colleagues are generalizing in a way that obscures the truth about themselves or others. For example, someone may assert that:

All the bosses in this place are obsessed with their own status.

No one in my position should make a mistake like that.

Every woman in the office is having an affair with someone.

When you are confronted with this sort of statement your most likely response is to challenge it with a counter-example. Take the first, for example:

You   I understand what you're saying, but let me just check it out. I know Rena turned down promotion not long ago because she was more interested in day-to-day project management. How does that tally with being obsessed with status?

Colleague That's true, but look at Rena. You'd hardly call her a 'boss' would you?

As the conversation goes on it becomes clear that the original assertion isn't factually true at all; it is true by definition. Your colleague has defined the term 'boss' in such a way that only those who are 'obsessed with their status' count as real bosses! No true manager can be anything *but* status obsessed.

The 'no true manager' move is one we all make from time to time, and recognizing it when it occurs can be an effective way of clarifying what is really at issue in a problem-solving discussion.

Before we move on to the next logical tool it is worth returning to the second example. We suggest you tackle the question we now want to put as an activity.

ACTIVITY 4.1

In what way could the 'no true manager' tool be helpful to someone making this assertion? What might you want to explore with a colleague making this assertion?

COMMENT

We would have wanted to challenge the assertion by suggesting instances in which others in that same position had made errors in the course of their work.

- Be ready for the response that these people were 'not really in my position'.
- Explore the meaning of 'in my position'.
- Be on the lookout for a definition of 'in my position' that meant 'in the position of someone who makes no errors'.

If–then thinking

One of the commonest sources of illogicality when assessing situations and events arises from a misapplication of the laws of premise and consequence. We call this if–then thinking. Here, in Case Study 4.1, is a demonstration of what we mean.

CASE STUDY 4.1: THE PRESENTATION

Faith is a successful sales manager, who regularly gives presentations to groups of 20–30 colleagues. Three months ago she experienced a panic attack during one of her presentations and has had the same feelings during two subsequent ones. She is clearly distressed at this development. Nothing like it has ever happened before and she has not panicked in any other situation. She explains to you: 'Every panic attack I've had occurs at a presentation . . . I just don't know what to do. "Give it up" is all I can think of.'

ACTIVITY 4.2

Can you see the logical mistake that has been made here? If so, how would you respond to the employee?

COMMENT

This study is a good example of if–then thinking. The mistake is based on a misunderstanding of logic.

It may be the case that every panic attack has been experienced at a presentation, but it doesn't logically follow that all presentations in the future must therefore be accompanied by panic attacks.

You could have reassured your employee in this way, perhaps drawing on a parallel example to show the fallacy involved. For example, just because all women have two eyes, it does not follow that all creatures with two eyes are women. Or because all repetitive strain injury results from word-processing that all word-processors lead to repetitive strain injury.

Expressed in schematic form we are saying that from the premise:

If A then B

it does not follow that:

If B then A

This fallacy is widespread in many thinking errors and you need to be on your guard for it, ready to challenge and dispel it whenever it occurs.

Drawing lines

How many times have you heard someone say, in a critical tone 'Where do you draw the line?' Well, where indeed? Sometimes it is impossible to draw a precise line. In these situations a particular distinction is often in question, e.g. between acceptable and unacceptable behaviour. The difficulty of precisely specifying the point at which the distinction comes into play is then cited against the validity of the distinction itself. Here, in Case Study 4.2, is a typical example.

 ## CASE STUDY 4.2

Sharon worked as a deputy manager in a small general store. She regularly helped herself to coffee from the store's shelves when taking her coffee break—a habit she had followed for several years. Recently a new member of staff, Anna, had joined as assistant to Sharon. Two weeks into her job she asked for a confidential discussion with the store manager:

Anna   I need to talk to you about Sharon – I'm a bit uneasy about her.

Manager   What particular thing do you feel uneasy with?

Anna   Well, she likes to have a morning cup of coffee, and I've noticed that instead of bringing in her own she just takes one off the shelf.

Manager   Without paying?

Anna   Yes – that's just it. I reckon that in the four years she's been here she must have got through about eighty jars. Now that's quite a sum. I don't like reporting people, but to me that's theft.

Manager   Theft's quite a strong word. I'd normally associate that with something more major – taking money from the till, for instance.

Anna   Yes, but what's the difference really? I mean, drinking the store's coffee, stealing from the till. Where do you draw the line?

Let's look at what's happening here. Anna is arguing that because it's hard to say exactly where use of the store's resources becomes theft, then any use of resources is theft. This may seem plausible at first sight, and in fact many people do argue in this way. But the move is logically flawed. Distinctions are not invalidated because they are difficult to draw. The philosopher Ludwig Wittgenstein noted that a balding man could never pinpoint a day on which, looking in the mirror, he could definitively state: 'Now I am bald.' Yet some people clearly are bald as opposed to hirsute. Similarly, turquoise does not prevent us describing things as blue or green.

Drawing lines is rarely simple, but it is often unnecessary. Most of the time we can live with fuzzy edges to our categories. In Anna's case, recognition that not all use of the store's resources counted as 'theft' enabled her to take a more tolerant view of Sharon's practice—which the store manager was quite prepared to tolerate, given that she was an able and conscientious member of staff. However, the manager realized that he needed to provide tea and coffee in the rest room to avoid any future misunderstandings. It is worth noting that in some organizations the staff manual would explicitly state that actions such as Sharon's would be considered as theft.

A note and a caution

Reductio ad absurdum is a time-honoured technique among lawyers and philosophers, and you can learn from it as a problem-solving manager. However, here the context is people problems. Although the logical tools in this section can all be used in an adversarial way, it is important to remember that your colleague is not your adversary. You have a common interest in tackling a problem, and although there may be times when challenge is appropriate (see below), your intention should never be to score points over the other person or expose their weakness—logical or otherwise.

Challenging illogical thinking

In any interview your initial aim will be to enable your colleague to speak freely and articulate their problem with a minimum of intervention from yourself. However, once you sense that the problem has been defined, your task is to help them to reassess their position. This may involve taking a critical attitude to a feeling, belief, or practice that they have long taken for granted. One of your key roles here is to initiate the process by challenging your colleague's unhelpful beliefs, attitudes, and behaviours, but *not* the person directly.

We need to emphasize that while challenging does involve confronting, it does not require you to take a confrontational attitude—indeed, this would almost certainly be quite counter-productive. We discuss what these challenges may be later in this chapter. But first, here are some general guidelines on challenging.

When using challenging skills:

I Check that you have developed mutual trust (sometimes described as 'earning the right to challenge').

2   Beware of reacting against views whose only 'shortcoming' is that they are not your own.
3   Offer challenges tentatively, bearing in mind that you may be wrong.
4   Make it clear that you are ready to be challenged yourself.
5   Encourage your colleague to challenge themselves, if possible.

Challenging the value of reactions

You will sometimes find it appropriate to ask your colleague to reflect on the purpose served by reacting in a particular—for example, an habitual—way. Looking at a situation from a purely functional point of view can be a very powerful tool for changing attitudes and values, especially the context of work. Let's look at Case Study 4.3.

 CASE STUDY 4.3

Lisa had worked for three years in the footwear department of a large department store. Her supervisor arranged a meeting of all staff working in footwear to discuss new working arrangements. When the arrangements had been explained, the supervisor gave the group a brief pep-talk, emphasizing how well the department was performing.

Later that day Lisa approached her supervisor looking deeply annoyed. Why, she asked, had she been treated this way. She resented being treated like a child. If new working arrangements were needed she didn't need a sweetener —a 'pat on the head'.

Lisa's supervisor refrained from reacting in a confrontational way, but instead questioned whether this was the only interpretation to be put on the pep-talk, and asked Lisa if she thought her reaction was helping her personally. The tentative nature of this challenge enabled Lisa to explore the question for herself over an intervening weekend. She was able to return to work on the Monday morning resolved to stand back a little from her immediate interpretation of events, particularly where her interpretation was a strongly negative one.

Challenging demands

Earlier we mentioned that demands such as 'musts', 'shoulds', 'oughts', 'have tos', and 'got tos' exacerbate stress. You may find the following questions useful when challenging this type of rigid and inflexible thinking:

Empirical

● Where is the evidence that you must . . .?
● Is there any evidence that you must . . .?
● Where is the law of the universe that states that you must . . .?
● Is there are law of the universe that states that you must . . .?
● If there were a law of the universe that stated that you must . . ., how do you account for the fact that you didn't do what the law dictated that you do?
● Would a scientist think there was any evidence in support of your must?

Logical

● Where is the logic that you must . . .?
● Is it logical to believe that you must . . .?
● Does it logically follow that because you want to . . . therefore you must . . .?
● Does that must logically follow from your preference?
● Is it good logic to believe that because you want to . . . therefore you must . . .?
● Would a philosopher think that it was good logic to believe that because you want to . . . therefore you must . . .?

Pragmatic

● Where will it get you to believe that you must . . .?
● What are the emotional and behavioural consequences of believing that you must . . .?

- Will that must give you good results?
- Is it healthy to believe that you must . . .?
- How is believing that you must . . . going to help you achieve your (long-term/healthy) goals?
- Is believing that you must . . . going to help or hinder you in the pursuit of your (long-term/healthy) goals?

Challenging exaggerations

Exaggerations form an important class of irrational beliefs. We have already given examples of these. They include statements like:

It's terrible/devastating/awful.

I can't stand it.

I'm a worthless person.

The checklist below summarizes some of the typical responses that you could use to challenge statements of this sort. This list is not intended to be a directory. The point of including it is to give you a clear sense of the way in which you can frame effective challenges. The particular form of words you choose will depend on the dynamics of the interview and your customary ways of talking to your colleague.

- What makes that awful/terrible/devastating?
- Is it really that awful?
- Just because it felt awful, how does it make it awful?
- Awful. Do you really mean that it was the end of the world?
- Can you think of anything worse?
- Is it really as bad as your finger dropping off?
- I can see that it was very bad but how does that make it awful?
- If you can't stand it, what do you think will happen to you?
- When you say that you can't stand it, what do you picture happening to you?

- Where is the evidence that you can't stand it?
- Surely you are living evidence that you have stood it for *x* years? Of course, you may have stood it miserably.
- Just because you made a mistake, how does it logically follow that you are totally useless/worthless?
- Where is the evidence that you are totally useless/worthless?

Challenging thinking errors

 ACTIVITY 4.3

As an alternative approach, you may wish to challenge thinking by working through the checklist opposite (Fig. 4.1) with your colleague. Ideally, pass a copy of it to them after an initial meeting. Ask them to work carefully through it, ticking the boxes on the right-hand side. Suggest they use a rating system, for example:

One tick	probably
Two ticks	certainly
Three ticks	absolutely right—bull's-eye

Eliminating distorted thinking

Where distorted thinking occurs, your role is to help your colleague eliminate it. The following plan is one possible way of proceeding. Use it with care and adapt it as necessary.

Identify the distortions

Copy the checklist opposite and ask your colleagues to write down any distortions they recognize.

Examine the evidence

Ask your colleague to assess what evidence exists for the negative thoughts.

Am I:

Jumping to conclusions? ☐

Mind-reading? ☐

Assuming my view of things is the only possible one? ☐

Posing questions that have no answers? ☐

Thinking in all-or-nothing terms? ☐

Using ultimatum words (musts/shoulds) in my thinking? ☐

Totally condemning myself (or someone else) on the basis of a single event? ☐

Concentrating on my weaknesses and neglecting my strengths? ☐

Blaming myself for something that is not really my fault? ☐

Taking things personally that have little or nothing to do with me? ☐

Expecting myself or others to be perfect? ☐

Using a double standard? ☐

Paying attention only to the negative side of things? ☐

Overestimating the chances of disaster? ☐

Exaggerating the importance of events? ☐

Fretting about how things should be instead of accepting and dealing with them as they are? ☐

Assuming that I cannot do anything to alter the situation? ☐

Predicting the outcome instead of experimenting with it? ☐

Fig. 4.1 Checklist for challenging distorted thinking

CASE STUDY 4.4

Christy came to her boss complaining that none of her colleagues ever helped her during busy periods in the fast-food restaurant where she worked. Her boss asked her to make a list of the things other staff actually did to help her.

Test out the thought

Ask your colleague to test the validity of their negative thought.

 CASE STUDY 4.5

Rod thought that he couldn't possibly take time off without his department grinding to a halt. His boss suggested that he could take two days off and check what actually happened.

Think in shades of grey

Ask your colleague to rate a situation, or parts of it, on a scale of 1–100.

 CASE STUDY 4.6

Rachel thought that her failure to pass an accountancy exam was an absolute disaster. Her boss suggested she rate different aspects of her situation on a 0–100 success scale.

Carry out a survey

Suggest a survey among colleagues to see if they concur with the negative view.

CASE STUDY 4.7

A sales rep in an insurance firm was feeling anxious about a presentation she was shortly to make. Her manager suggested she ask others about their own reactions in similar circumstances. Would they feel equally anxious? If she failed to make the impact she intended, would they see her as a complete failure?

Define emotive terms

If a colleague uses emotive terms such as 'berk', 'idiot', 'bastard', or 'asshole' to label themselves or others, ask them to explain what these terms really mean. For example, would a total idiot ever succeed in getting to work in the first place?

 CASE STUDY 4.8

Emma was angry with herself for missing a mistake on the title page of a book she had edited and passed to the printer. 'I feel like a complete and utter fool', she explained tearfully. The senior editor asked her to examine her terms more closely. Would a complete fool have been able to manage the rest of the production process so skilfully? Or would someone so incompetent be so concerned about making an error like this in the first place? She may have acted foolishly but how does that make her a complete fool?

Translate the absolutes

If your colleague is using extreme or absolute terms, especially 'musts', 'shoulds', 'oughts', 'have tos', and 'got tos', encourage them to substitute less extreme, relative ones.

CASE STUDY 4.9

Angus had sent a letter to his staff requesting them to attend an evening training session. He had included the words 'Attendance is not optional. I will only accept apologies in writing, which must come to me six days in advance.' Since the training was to be carried out in the staff's own time the letter had resulted in considerable resentment. Angus was encouraged to see the value of reformulating this and other requests into less absolute terms. For example, his next letter included the phrase 'I would very much like you to attend this session, but if you are unable to do so please send me a written note at least six days beforehand to assist in planning.'

Reattribute the blame

Encourage colleagues to assess all the factors that have led to a problem situation.

CASE STUDY 4.10

An asthma patient had died during the night on a hospital ward. The staff nurse was convinced that she could have done more to help. By taking a problem-solving approach, her manager helped her to see that there was a variety of factors in the situation. Some of these were outside her control at the time. By re-viewing the situation in this way she was able to feel remorse instead of self-defeating guilt and also to take a constructive approach to help ensure that a similar situation was less likely to occur in the future.

Carry out a cost–benefit analysis

Ask your colleague to assess the value of their unhelpful beliefs and unhealthy, negative feelings or behaviour.

CASE STUDY 4.11

Brad's problem was presentations. In discussion with his manager it soon became clear that he frequently found himself thinking, 'I must give a superb presentation; everyone's got to be really impressed—otherwise things will be awful.' As a result he tended to feel anxious, and then tended to put off vital planning in advance of the event. With his manager's encouragement he listed the pros and cons of his thinking, and was able to see his situation more clearly. Here is how his analysis looked.

Irrational belief: I *must* give a superb presentation

Pros	Cons
I'll strive to do my best.	I will spend all my spare time thinking about my presentation.
If I do well I'll be really happy about myself.	I am making myself anxious and I will be less likely to perform well. Then I will put myself down.
My boss will be impressed.	If I carry on feeling so anxious I might mess up the presentation and then she's likely to think less well of me.
At least my desk is tidy.	I'm so worried about performing well that I can't concentrate on preparation, and I find myself wasting valuable time tidying up my desk.

We suggest you use a similar sort of analysis when you are dealing with people problems—perhaps using the example above as the model for a ready-made cost–benefit form (see Figs. 4.2 and 4.3 on pp 88 and 89).

Irrational belief …

… …

… …

Advantages	Disadvantages

NB: An irrational belief consists of a rigid and unqualified must, should, have to, got to, ought, and a derivative which is usually 'awfulizing', 'I-can't-stand-it-itis' or damnation of self and/or others.

Fig. 4.2 Irrational belief: cost–benefit form

Rational belief ... ...
Advantages / **Disadvantages**
NB: A rational belief consists of a flexible preference, wish, want, desire, and a derivative which is usually 'de-awfulizing', 'I can stand it' or acceptance of self and/or others.

Fig. 4.3   Rational belief: cost–benefit form

Challenge and trust

We hope that the importance of trust has been implicit in much of what we have said so far; and we emphasize the importance of self-awareness in Chapter 7 on pages 177–180. Precisely how you build up trust is, ultimately, up to you, but here are some brief pointers and examples.

Offer challenges tentatively

Not: 'You say you work well on your own but I've often seen you wasting time gossiping.'

But: 'You say you work well on your own. I wonder how that squares with my observation that you enjoy a good chat now and again.'

Make it clear that you are ready to be challenged yourself

Not: 'You're taking a quite unjustified view of Mark's behaviour.'

But: 'You may want to correct me, but I wonder whether there are more positive ways of looking at Mark's behaviour?'

Encourage your colleague to challenge themselves, if possible

Not: 'I can't see what you can gain from reacting like that.'

But: 'How is it benefiting you behaving in that manner?'

Challenging beliefs

The distinction between espoused beliefs and beliefs-in-practice has two very useful roles in the *challenging phase* of the problem-solving interview. You may wish to:

● Challenge a negative espoused belief by pointing to positive beliefs-in-practice.
● Challenge a positive espoused belief by pointing to negative beliefs-in-practice.

Let's look at each of these in turn.

Challenging negative espoused beliefs

Suppose that in the course of questioning your colleague espouses a negative belief about themselves. For example, they might say something like:

1 I couldn't possibly help with the launch. I'm just not a mixing sort of person.
2 I could never do a presentation. Standing up in front of a crowd of people would terrify me.
3 This interview isn't going to get us anywhere. Talking things over can't help someone in my position.

 ACTIVITY 4.4

In each of these cases you could, through further questioning, establish a fundamental assumption—an espoused belief—that is driving these negative statements.

Spend a few moments thinking about this. What might the assumptions be in each case. Note down your response, bearing in mind that there is no right or wrong answer in each case.

 COMMENT

Our own suggestions are as follows. Don't worry if your suggestions are very different, provided that you have grasped the basic principle.

Statement	Espoused belief
1 I couldn't possibly help with the launch.	I'm just not a mixing sort of person.
2 I could never do a presentation.	Standing up to speak in front of a crowd would terrify me.

Statement	Espoused belief
3 This interview isn't going to get us anywhere.	Talking things over can't help someone in my position.

Identifying beliefs in practice

Once you have elicited the espoused belief you are in a position to challenge it by exploring beliefs-in-practice, using the guidelines for dialogue we have suggested in Chapter 2. In the three examples we have been discussing the results might be on the following lines.

I'm not a mixing sort of person

Abby, the person who said this, turned out to enjoy a full social life with her local sports group, and was often the life and soul of family gatherings. Her belief-in-practice was that she was a highly competent social performer. Her special pleading was that work events were different and that more was expected of her there. In fact her own expectations were much higher than those of her managers. Once she was able to dispel these the result was a very successful launch in which Abby played a full part.

Standing up to speak in front of a crowd would terrify me

Ronald turned out to have sung with his local amateur operatic society in the past, and had not given a second thought to going on stage. His belief-in-practice was that he was a fully competent performer in front of a crowd. His special pleading was that he was happy if he had a prepared script that he could memorize in advance. Once it was pointed out that this was possible for his presentation, instead of feeling very anxious he felt concerned and was able to concentrate on preparing for the event.

Talking things over can't help someone in my position

Further discussion with Juan revealed that he had in the past confided frequently with his sister, who had been a major source of support. His belief-in-practice was 'It's good to talk.' His special pleading was that this was a work situation, and talking to close relatives was different. By clarifying the aims of the interview and its boundaries, Juan's manager was able to reassure Juan and move on to tackle the problem that he needed to resolve.

Challenging negative beliefs-in-practice

You can use a similar strategy for discerning and then challenging negative beliefs-in-practice. Since we have already looked at the detail of the strategy, we'll take a more summary approach here.

The need to challenge a negative belief-in-practice arises typically in situations where your interviewee is contributing to their own or others' problems by their actions, but is unaware of what they are doing. Here, in Case Studies 4.12 and 4.13, are two examples; you will almost certainly be able to find others from your own experience.

 ## CASE STUDY 4.12

Val came to her supervisor to complain that she was being cold-shouldered by others in the machine shop. It had got to the point where she was quite upset at what she saw as entirely unjustified treatment.

Her supervisor was able to establish that Val's colleagues had told her they felt she was very critical of them. Val had very strong religious views which didn't square with some of the language and behaviour of her colleagues. 'But they are so wrong', said Val, 'I believe everyone has a right to their own views. Judge not and ye shall not be judged.'

By careful questioning Val's supervisor was able to challenge her espoused belief, and helped Val see that her actions tended to give a very different impression to those with whom she was working.

CASE STUDY 4.13

Martin was a middle manager in a large life assurance company. He was suffering from stress. Everyone could see that, including Martin. He looked permanently harassed and he had taken up smoking again, after kicking the habit six or seven years previously. His manager decided it was time to intervene.

It became clear to Martin's manager that the source of his stress was chronic overwork. Martin was mystified by this. Other managers in the company were just as productive and seemed to be less fraught, and he was sure that he was working efficiently. And 'I'm a great believer in delegation' he explained.

Martin's manager decided to explore the espoused belief about delegation. Martin had a degree from a well-known business school, and was well aware of good management practice. But his manager was right: the espoused commitment was very different to what was actually happening. Martin delegated only relatively unimportant tasks as he believed 'I must be in control at all times.' Once Martin was able to recognize this contradiction he was ready to start planning a strategy to reduce his chronic overwork and make the most of his very wide-ranging skills.

Summary

This brings us to the end of our survey of essential thinking skills. Bear in mind that you will need to practise these over several dialogues before you can deploy them spontaneously in response to a situation—so make a point of regularly returning to this chapter for a refresher.

In the next chapter we look at a seven-stage agenda for problem solving. Thoughts and feelings will be recurring themes in what follows, as will the ABCDE framework. Each short subsection will focus on one stage of the seven-stage agenda and we will be cross-referencing the text to some of the key skills that have been covered earlier in the book.

References

Burns, D. D. (1989) *The Feeling Good Handbook,* William Morrow, New York, United States of America.

Dryden, W. (1994) *Overcoming Guilt,* Sheldon Press, London.

Dryden, W. (1995) *Facilitating Client Change in Rational Emotive Behaviour Therapy,* Whurr, London.

Dryden, W. and Gordon, J. (1990) *Think Your Way to Happiness,* Sheldon, London.

Dryden, W. and Gordon, J. (1995) *Think Rationally: A Brief Guide to Overcoming Your Emotional Problems,* Centre for Rational Emotive Behaviour Therapy, London.

Dryden, W. and Gordon, J. (1993) *Peak Performance: Become More Effective at Work,* Mercury Business Books, Didcot.

Ellis, A. (1988) *How to Stubbornly Refuse to Make Yourself Miserable About Anything—Yes Anything!,* Lyle Stuart, Secaucus, NJ, United States of America.

Epictetus (1890) *The Collected Works of Epictetus,* Little, Brown, Boston, MA, United States of America.

Hauck, P. (1980) *Depression,* Sheldon Press, London.

Marcus Aurelius. (1890) *Meditations,* Little, Brown, Boston, MA, United States of America.

Palmer, S. and Dryden, W. (1995) *Counselling for Stress Problems,* Sage, London.

Palmer, S. and Strickland, L. (1995) *Stress Management: A Quick Guide,* Folens, Dunstable, Bedfordshire.

CHAPTER 5

The people problems agenda

Introduction

The next part of this book introduces a seven-stage agenda for dealing with people problems. By working through this part of the book you will find out how to help colleagues take a constructive approach to their own problems and also how to use the seven-stage agenda to deal with your own problems in the workplace.

Seven stages of problem solving

The seven stages on which this part of the book is based are shown in Fig. 5.1. These seven stages provide a simple agenda for tackling a wide range of people problems. They can be applied over a period of time, or in the space of a single meeting, and may involve discussion at varying degrees of depth. In other words: be flexible!

Each of the sections that follows focuses on a specific stage in the agenda, using a variety of case studies. Each stage also calls for particular skills, which we introduce by way of short activities. As we emphasized at the start, it is important to take the time to build up these skills, and within each section we suggest ways in which they can usefully be practised in isolation, before you begin to assemble them into a seamless whole. In doing this you will be doing no more or less than a pianist who learns to play each hand separately first, while playing a satisfying tune with each hand individually.

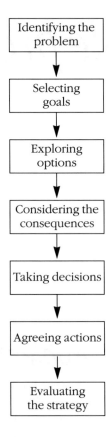

Fig. 5.1   Seven stages of problem solving

Stage 1: Identifying the problem

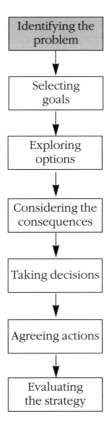

Fig. 5.2   Identifying the problem

Here we assume you have encountered a people problem in your workplace.
The problem could have presented itself to you:

● Directly—a colleague could have requested a meeting with you.
● Directly—you observe members of your team being unable to work
  together.

● Indirectly—someone could have drawn your attention to a problem being experienced by a colleague.

In the first phase of your discussion with your colleague your main aim will be to gain as clear an understanding as possible of the issues as they see them.

Understanding the issues

At the outset, the real problem may be far from clear. Here are three examples which illustrate this point.

 ## CASE STUDY 5.1

Geoff came to have a short chat with his supervisor, Alan. When Alan asked what the problem was, Geoff simply said 'I don't know really. Things just don't seem to be going right for me at the moment.' Then he fell silent.

 ## CASE STUDY 5.2

Tom found Lisa sitting in his office one afternoon when he returned from lunch. She looked gloomy. 'Do you want to talk?' he enquired. 'Not really. I've just got some secretary problems', was Lisa's response.

 ## CASE STUDY 5.3

Andrew asked Tayyeb for an urgent meeting. He came in looking flustered and shut the door sharply behind him. 'I don't know where to begin. There's so much. It's all suddenly got on top of me. I just seem to be in one stinking great mess.'

In situations like this your first task is to help your colleague clarify what the issue is. Bear in mind that this lack of clarity may have several causes.

● There may be genuine confusion about what is wrong—perhaps a general sense of unease or anxiety.
● The problems may seem too complex: it may be difficult to know where to begin.
● There may be some reluctance to disclose what the problem is.

In fact, the chances are that there will be a mixture of all these factors.

Whatever the mix is, your joint task is to map out the issues as clearly as possible. Clarity really is paramount. If your colleague, or you, are unable to define the issues, it is unlikely to be worthwhile continuing at this stage.

Clarifying techniques

Let's assume that you have a clear sense of what your colleague thinks and feels. Your next task is to use clarifying techniques to help them reach a point where they can take positive action to solve their problems.

Achieving clarity involves more than responding with the right form of words. In the early stages of problem solving you may frequently encounter a bewildering range of interpersonal issues. This can result in such confusion that a solution seems difficult to envisage. As one manager complained 'I'm sure that I could deal with most of the people problems in work, but so often I just don't seem to be able to get a lever on the situation.' Yet, as we have emphasized, clarity and mutual understanding are vital if real progress is to be made.

There is, of course, no single way of guaranteeing this. But you can still deploy a range of useful techniques to assist both yourself and your colleagues to gain a clearer understanding of the real nature of interpersonal issues. We have already looked at one key technique: inference chaining (see pages 66–69). Here we want to supplement this with further suggestions. But first, three important principles.

Externalize, visualize, simplify

The techniques we recommend for stage I are based on three underlying principles which have been shown by psychologists to be of value in problem solving.

Externalizing

Externalizing involves displaying information visually wherever possible. By doing this you free the mind from the need to present data and free it to put energy into the more critical activities of interpreting and evaluating. In practical terms this may mean using a notepad, flip-chart or even an overhead projector to illustrate or map out the problem scenario, sharing your notes with those of your colleague or member of staff.

Visualizing

Researchers have found that information presented visually is more likely to be understood and remembered. Maps, charts, and diagrams can show interrelationships far more effectively than purely verbal notes, and a person who actively visualizes a problem situation in their mind is likely to be able to describe it more accurately and in more depth.

Simplifying

A complex problem becomes more manageable if broken down into sub-problems; similarly, complex or vague ideas become clearer when translated into simpler and more concrete terms.

Bear these three principles in mind at every stage of your work as a problem-solver, and particularly at this initial stage of identifying the problem. The following techniques are specific ways of doing this.

Mapping people problems

First we want to introduce you to the problem planogram developed by Stephen Palmer. This simple system of mapping interpersonal issues has been used successfully in stress management and can be readily adapted to tackling generic people problems.

A problem planogram is a powerful way of plotting problems created in the workplace. It aids problem assessment and can help you and your colleague to understand a complex situation.

● The severity of the problem is rated on a scale of 0–10 where 10 represents an extremely severe problem and 0 represents an absence of any problem.
● A + sign represents a frequent peak to a more severe problem.
● Arrowheads show the direction from which the stress, tensions, or conflict are coming.

Figure 5.3 shows the basic form of a typical planogram, with the problem owner in the centre.

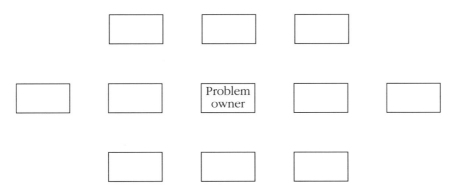

Fig. 5.3   Problem planogram

Here is how you could use the device in practice.

 CASE STUDY 5.4

Alvina, a 43-year-old lecturer, had been finding her work trying for several months. She found her job stressful but was unclear why, especially as she seemed to get on well with other staff. At her annual appraisal meeting with

Paul, the departmental head, she explained her feelings of stress and anxiety. Paul suggested she draw up a problem planogram. The result was as shown in Fig. 5.4. From this the following points emerged:

● Alvina perceived John and Hank as the cause of her problems.
● Alvina believed John was causing problems among his own students—a fact she was aware of because she had been informally counselling two of them for several weeks.
● John's behaviour was also bringing him into conflict with Hank, who was passing on his irritation to Alvina—hence the flare-ups between herself and Hank in an otherwise fairly equable relationship.

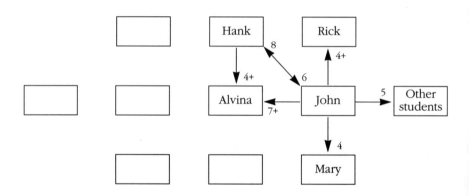

Fig. 5.4 Alvina's problem planogram

Using the planogram, Alvina was therefore able to get to grips with a potentially complex situation and identify the sources of her stress at work. However, the plan still has one major component missing. At this stage it shows only the effect that Alvina perceived others had on her. After further discussion with Paul she added further lines and numbers to show the effect she perceived herself having on others. The resulting planogram is shown in Fig. 5.5. Note that not all the boxes have been filled, leaving open the possibility of further development.

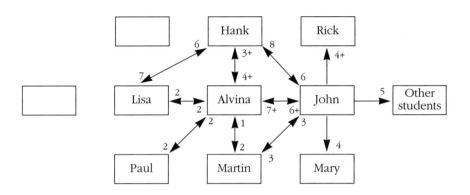

Fig. 5.5 Alvina's completed problem planogram

The planogram demonstrated to Alvina that some of the relationship problems which previously seemed beyond her control were partly an indirect result of her own behaviour, and so were within her power to resolve.

 ## ACTIVITY 5.1

To familiarize yourself with the planogram technique we suggest you try it out for yourself. Take your own working environment and map out the sources of people problems as you perceive them, using appropriate symbols.

As a further development of this activity you could work with a colleague. Prepare planograms for the same working environment and then compare notes. Ask yourselves:

● On what points do we concur?
● On what points do we diverge?
● What could account for the divergences?

COMMENT

Bear in mind that the results of your activity are not a definitive diagnosis of the problems in your workplace and their origins. The problem planogram makes no claim to objectivity. Its value is:

● For the person experiencing problems, to clarify their view of their situation.
● For you, in dealing with people problems, to see the world from their perspective and to comprehend the often complex web of relationships that characterize their working life.

Once the initial planogram has been prepared it can serve as a reference point during further explorations. These may sometimes challenge the plan or suggest revisions to it. For example, in Alvina's case, it might subsequently emerge that although she perceived John as a source of tension for his students, one student in particular was making tutoring difficult for John and this was reflected in his irritation with other, more demanding students. It could be that due to cutbacks John was now working longer hours.

Listing people problems

Planograms work best when the problem involves a network of relationships in the workplace. Irrational beliefs, new computers, government regulations, and other difficulties can also be included on a planogram. However, there are many problem situations in which other factors also come into play, and in these circumstances a planogram may not be the most effective tool. In exploring this sort of problem you may find it useful simply to compile a list detailing all the issues that you and your colleague have identified. Here is an example of the sort of list that might emerge from a problem-solving discussion.

CASE STUDY 5.5

A 49-year-old electrical salesperson had come to visit his boss following notice that he was shortly to be fired. His initial problem had been absenteeism over several afternoons. Colleagues had reported seeing him sitting alone in a local park. After an interview with his boss the following problem list was drawn up.

● Loss of job: job will soon go in company-wide reorganization
● Low self-acceptance
● Isolation from colleagues
● Depression—worst at weekends
● Loss of interest in leisure activities
● Difficulty with sharing feelings with wife: she is reluctant to be drawn into problems

Prioritizing problems

Once the problems have been listed, you may find it helpful to jointly rate these in order of priority. Prioritizing can enable you to identify:

● The degree of interdependence between problems
● A priority order for tackling these

Here is the same list of problems again, this time in order of priority. Notice that 'loss of job' in fact comes last. This is inevitable. There is no way to avoid it, except by a longer-term job-finding strategy. In the meantime the situation needs to be accepted for what it is, with a focus on repairing the emotional damage.

1 Low self-acceptance
2 Depression—worst at weekends
3 Isolation from colleagues
4 Loss of interest in leisure activities

5 Difficulty with sharing feelings with wife: she is reluctant to be drawn into problems.
6 Loss of job

Summary

Step 1 involves exploring the nature of the presenting problem and homing in on the one on which a problem-solving strategy can be focused. You can do this either by mapping and prioritizing—in the case of a range of presenting problems—or by inference chaining—in the case of a single presenting problem. Or you can use both strategies in tandem, pinpointing the key problem first and then using inference chaining to explore the unreasonable beliefs that power it.

Finally, note one very simple additional technique. Sometimes you may find that if instead of asking 'What is the problem?' you ask 'What would you like to change?' you will be given concrete answers that help to clarify the situation.

You are now ready to move on to step 2 and explore ways of generating goals for problem solving.

Stage 2: Selecting goals

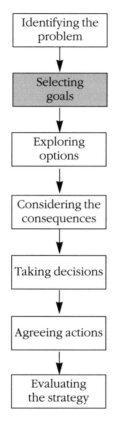

Fig. 5.6 Selecting goals

Introduction

You have now had identified the problem that your colleague wishes to tackle. This may have been in a previous discussion, perhaps two or three days ago, or it may have been at an earlier point in the same discussion.

Your aim is now to help your colleague to set realistic goals for themselves. We will show you how this can be done in terms of:

● Emotion
● Behaviour

You will also need to challenge goals that seem unrealistic—while acknowledging that the final decision in setting goals should always rest with your colleague.

You will now be aware of:

● The range of the problem
● The key people and issues involved
● The relative importance of the range of interconnected issues

Your next task is to help your colleague to define and select their goals.

What goals shall I select?

We have now emphasized a range of considerations to bear in mind when you are exploring goals or change with your colleague. Your ultimate aim is to draw up a shortlist of up to three or four goals for serious consideration.

We have already looked at the importance of working within the client's capabilities, including their personal and environmental resources. In addition, check that any solutions identified are:

● Specific
● Realistic
● Substantial
● Verifiable
● Recognized by your colleague as their own, whether originally from yourself or from them

Let's unpack what these terms mean in practice. Throughout this short section we'll take the example of an employee who has developed a tendency to panic while giving presentations to colleagues.

Specific

'Tackle my negative features' is hopelessly unspecific as a goal. 'Tackle my negative self-talk' is better, but you might still question what 'tackle' might really amount to. A finally refined, realistic goal could be 'To give an adequate presentation to the sales team.'

Realistic

'Give a one-hour presentation tomorrow without panicking' may well be taking things too far too quickly. An initial goal probably needs to be less ambitious and less instant. Encourage your colleague to take things step-by-step and at a realistic pace. In this case a more productive goal may be 'Speak to the sales team for ten minutes next week.' This achievement can then be built on over a period of weeks until a full hour's session is achieved.

Substantial

In setting goals that are realistic, beware of aiming too low. Continuing with the example of a presentation, it would be feasible, but not very helpful, to set as a goal 'Meet the sales team for an informal discussion.' Even if this is successful, it may not be a substantial enough achievement to give your colleague a sense of real progress towards the goal of no longer panicking at a major presentation.

Verifiable

It helps if both you and your colleague have a clear sense of what the goal that has been set really amounts to in observable, behavioural terms. That way you will be able to judge how far it has been achieved. So 'Feel more relaxed during a presentation' is unhelpful until your colleague articulates what 'feeling more relaxed' amounts to—e.g. less tension in the stomach, slower heartbeat, slower breathing, fewer images of failure.

Recognized as their own

Goals that motivate need to be your colleague's own—that is, they need to be:

- At best, suggested by them.
- At worst, suggested by you but fully in line with their own aspirations and values.

Ownership of goals is vital. Unless someone is personally committed to a goal—pursuing it as a result of their freely given commitment—they are unlikely to devote to it the personal resources necessary for its attainment.

The Swiss cheese

There may be times when a colleague's problems seem almost too complex even to prioritize. Just which goals do you select? In this situation we suggest the 'Swiss cheese' approach.

This may sound flippant, but it isn't. You know Swiss cheeses? The ones that are riddled with holes? Picture the mass of problem issues as an unholy cheese, and take a gradual, hole-making approach to them, burrowing into the mass in one place and then another. Take one aspect of the mass of problems and together work out a strategy for tackling just that. If you need to prioritize, choose one where you both feel there is a chance of making some headway. Complete tasks and review progress. The very fact of progress with one small burrow into the Swiss cheese—even if this represents a relatively insignificant aspect of the problem—is likely to make the overall cheese seem less intimidating. And the chances are that the more you burrow, the more the problem will shrink and the more your colleague's morale will increase.

 CASE STUDY 5.6: Christine

Christine had recently had a rather negative performance review. She was making a lot of errors in her work as a software technician, and her productivity had sunk to an all-time low. Her manager suggested an exploratory chat to discuss any wider issues. It soon became clear that Christine was in a very anxious and confused state. Six months ago she had moved into an apartment with her boyfriend of several years, and they had agreed to share all financial commitments. Things had rapidly begun to go wrong. Her boyfriend had become possessive and had at one point threatened Christine with violence. She had moved out of the apartment to live with her widowed mother, but her boyfriend had remained in the apartment and refused to leave. Christine could not afford the mortgage herself and was unable to agree with her boyfriend any way of settling the issue of which of the two should live in the apartment. Meanwhile her mother had lost her own job and was becoming dependent on Christine, financially and emotionally. The result was a situation in which, as Christine explained, she felt an increasing prisoner of her situation. In fact, she confided that she had a recurring image of herself actually sitting at home with her mother in a room with barred windows. Consequently her work was suffering and the performance review had left her anxious about her own job. She was beginning to have difficulty sleeping . . .

You may be confronted with a problem of this sort only rarely, or not at all. However, in this sort of situation, bear in mind the Swiss cheese. If even prioritizing action seems impossibly difficult, don't undervalue the strategy of doing just something: of making an initial, exploratory burrow into the cheese.

Refining the Swiss cheese

There are two important points we need to make in connection with the Swiss cheese. First, when selecting an initial issue to tackle you will need to bear in mind the limits of your own competence as a problem-solver. An effective strategy may include referral—a point which we develop further on page 174–176.

Second, where a mass of interconnected issues present themselves, you may find it helpful to put some structure into them by:

● The mapping technique we suggest on page 102–106.
● The BASIC.ID model, which you will find explained in the 'Wider issues' section on page 165–168.

Once the tangle is seen in a more systematic light you may find it less difficult to identify priorities, or at least one positive, solution-focused action.

 ACTIVITY 5.2

Pause for a moment now and see if you can apply the Swiss cheese technique to Christine's situation. You will need to use your imagination, but see if you can think of one or two initial strategies that are likely to start yielding positive results fairly quickly.

 COMMENT

Here's what actually happened.

Christine first agreed to try visualizing a positive mental image each time she caught herself picturing her 'prison scene'. At the same time her manager was able to point her in the direction of a legal aid centre to find out the real facts about the legal position with her apartment. Once she had a clear understanding of her financial rights, her morale improved noticeably, and she felt able to meet her boyfriend on neutral territory and agree a way forward. Then she joined a local carers' support group, which dispelled some of her fears about isolation with her mother.

Summary

You have now helped your colleague select one or more goals at which to aim, and ensured that these are framed in the most realistic and helpful way possible. You have also considered ways of working with a range of goals. The next stage is to help your colleague or member of staff identify possible ways of reaching the goals that have been selected.

Stage 3: Exploring options

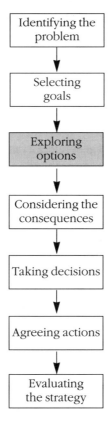

Fig. 5.7   Exploring options

Introduction

You have now agreed realistic goals with your colleague, expressed in a form that is going to be helpful both to themselves and to you. The next task is to encourage your colleague to think of possible ways of reaching these goals. In doing this it is essential to keep as open a mind as possible, and to allow for the possibility of unorthodox or previously unthought of solutions.

A stage 3 skill

We have already outlined a wide range of skills that you can deploy as a problem-solving manager. At the third stage in the problem-solving process you will continue to draw on these, and you can usefully add a further one to your inventory: brainstorming. If this skill is already familiar to you, pass over this section. If not, read on.

Brainstorming

Brainstorming is a simple way of generating a range of alternatives in response to any particular issue, challenge, or problem.

  ACTIVITY 5.3

We suggest you try brainstorming for yourself as you read each of the steps that follows. Pick your own issue, or use the following as an example:

> You have driven your car to the station and left it there to attend a meeting in a nearby city. When you return you find that you have left your keys behind in the meeting room.

Step 1

Identify the issue and frame it in the form of a question. Make a note of the question at the top of a sheet of paper.

● How can I get home with my car?

Step 2

Allow yourself 5–10 minutes to suggest of all possible responses to the question. Put down every response that suggests itself, no matter how far fetched, unrealistic, or frivolous these might seem on further reflection. Give your critical faculties a vacation for the duration you have set yourself. In this way you will give your creativity free rein and perhaps come across innovative solutions that you would otherwise have dismissed out of hand.

Step 3

Now, and only now, critically review your suggestions. It's likely that some of those you might have been tempted to dismiss will in fact be well worth considering, or are at the very least worth building on.

 COMMENT

Here is a typical list generated in response to the above question: How can I get home with my car?

- Get it airlifted by helicopter.
- Have it pushed by a bulldozer.
- Ask someone with a similar car to try their key in my lock.
- Chainsaw the roof off.
- Take a cab home, pick up the spare key, and come straight back.
- Borrow a hammer and smash open the door.
- Ring the police and have them break in.
- Ask Captain Kirk to dematerialize and transmit it.
- Take a cab home, then wait for my partner to bring me back in with the key.

And here is the shortlist of realistic suggestions:

- Ask someone with a similar car to try their key in my lock.
- Take a cab home, pick up the spare key, and come straight back.
- Take a cab home, then wait for my partner to bring me back in with the key.

Any of these might be feasible, and might not have suggested themselves without the brainstorm.

Resist the temptation to dismiss the first step as silly. The point about brainstorming is that it releases our creativity, which routinely tends to be blocked by a tendency to self-censoring. This self-censoring tends to be based on familiarity rather than innovation and can greatly inhibit the generation of solutions.

Reviewing resources

In order to make a realistic assessment of options your first task is to help your colleague identify their own resources. There is a clear logic for this. The problem-solving manager encourages others to use their existing strengths and supports as far as possible. They will be wary of posing the additional challenge of learning new skills and developing new support systems at a time when their colleague's ability to do so is particularly limited.

Exploring personal strengths

Here your key concerns should be:

● Have any similar problems been encountered in the past?

If the answer is yes, you probe further by questions such as:

– How did you cope with them?
– What strategies worked best?
– What strategies worked less well?

If a closely analogous situation presents itself you may find it helpful to probe further and ask for a detailed description. If your colleague protests that the problem they are now facing is uniquely difficult, you may be able to tactfully challenge their conception, using some of the clarifying strategies identified in pp. 101–108.

● Has past coping included avoidance strategies, such as alcohol abuse or absenteeism?

If your colleague has a marked tendency to side-step problems in this way, you may need to work on this behaviour—e.g. by asking them to reflect on its overall value to them.

- Did it help them solve their problem?
- What did the problem look like when they returned to it?
- Did it result in further problems?
- Did it provide them with the satisfaction that they had hoped for?

● How far does their current state of mind enable them to utilize past strengths? Evidence of past successes in problem solving will be to little avail if a person feels that their mental state is too fragile to repeat the success. You will need to register any ways in which their mental energy may be sapped by, for example, difficulty in sleeping or anxiety. If these are in evidence they will form part of the problem scenario rather than an element in its solution.

● How able is the person to come up with their own solutions? At this stage you will find it useful to begin exploring the degree to which the person is able to generate their own solutions. You might, for example, ask questions such as:

- Have you any ideas about how you might tackle this problem?

We take up the last point in more detail shortly.

Exploring personal supports

There are two particular forms of personal support that you can look out for in helping your colleague to assess their own support networks. These are as follows:

● *Emotional support*   Try to find out whether your colleague has a close family member, friend, or work associate with whom they feel able to discuss their problem. If so, it may be useful to suggest that they make a point of doing so, perhaps as part of an explicit arrangement. If your organization operates a mentoring system, explore how far a mentor could play a part in the problem-solving strategy.

● *Specialist support*   We discuss specialist psychological support under 'referral' in Chapter 7. Here we are concerned with the possible expert sources of help that your colleague can call on in tackling specific problems—from financial advice to time-management consultants.

Mapping support networks

One of the simplest but most effective ways of identifying sources of support is to prepare a simple map showing the support networks. This can be in any form that your colleague finds convenient. One simple device is a spider diagram, with the originator at the centre and the network spreading out from this point. Thicker lines can be used to indicate strength of support; longer lines can be used to indicate accessibility. Figure 5.8 was drawn up by an

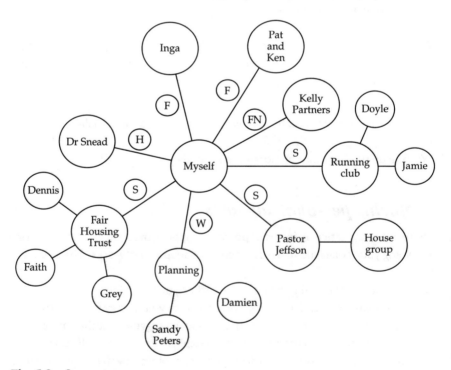

Fig. 5.8   Support map

employee experiencing severe stress as the result of promotion to a
demanding and exposed post within a PR firm. He has used a code to indicate
the different sorts of support:

F   family
FN   financial
S   social
H   health
W   workplace

  ## ACTIVITY 5.4

You may find it helpful at this point to prepare your own support diagram,
identifying resources you can call upon in dealing with people problems at
work. When your diagram is complete ask yourself:

● Was the amount of support available more or less than I had assumed, or
  about the same?
● Are there any gaps in my support network? If so, how am I going to plug
  these?
● What effect did compiling the diagram have on my sense of personal
  competence as a problem-solver?

 ## COMMENT

We suspect that you were pleasantly surprised by this activity. Most of us have
access to a wider range of support than we initially suppose. For a person
experiencing problems in the workplace, carrying out an activity of this sort
can have a very positive effect on their self-esteem. But even if support seems
thin, the activity of mapping deficits is itself a critical step in the path to
regaining control and developing workable solutions.

ACTIVITY 5.5

Think back to the last time you had a difficult workplace problem. Did you receive support from anybody in your support diagram? If not, why not?

Exploring environmental supports

So far we have focused on human support. And this is often as far as mapping of support systems goes. However, environmental factors can be critical in enhancing personal effectiveness in tackling work-based problems. They include any material factors that contribute to a person's overall quality of life, particularly where these are a source of self-acceptance.

The prompt lists following Activity 5.6 highlight potential environmental supports to look out for in working with colleagues to solve problems. The lists cover two specific types of support that have been identified as particularly effective: stability zones and rituals. Stability zones are the physical areas, belongings, or objects that an individual may be particularly fond of or accustomed to, which help promote their sense of well-being. Rituals are enjoyable routines or less regular habits which are a positive influence in a person's life. (So note that we are discounting ritual in the sense of 'obsessive behaviour', which far from being supportive may be a sign of deeper psychological disturbance.)

Aim to help your colleague identify:

● Supports that they have found helpful in the past but that have fallen into disuse.
● Current supports that they underutilize.
● New areas of support that they could develop.

 ACTIVITY 5.6

Write up your own list of stability zones and rituals. Which ones help you to unwind and relax?

Prompt list for stability zones

Examples of stability zones include:

● *Home*—rooms, areas within rooms, favourite chair, bath.
● *Workplace*—areas within workplace, desk, canteen, car.
● *Countryside*—places, landscapes, leisure facilities, forests, hills.
● *Town*—shops, services (e.g. hairdressers, restaurants), leisure facilities.
● *Other*—places of worship, parks, beach, cliff paths.

Prompt list for rituals/routines

● *Daily*—walking the dog, morning cup of tea or coffee, newspapers, listening to favourite radio programme, watching the news.
● *Weekly*—Sunday outings, eating out, weekend breaks, sports activities.
● *Annual*—vacations, anniversaries, social visits.

You will need to use this listing sensitively, bearing in mind that in some instances the real problem for an individual may be the irretrievable loss of important sources of stability. In this case your aim will be to assist them in identifying suitable compensations. The following example shows how this has worked in practice.

 CASE STUDY 5.7

A mail order firm in the north of England had recently undergone a period of substantial change, resulting in the downsizing of its orders department. The postal clerk had worked there for nearly 20 years, coming in to work at 10.00 a.m. and overseeing two dispatches of mail before leaving at 4.00 p.m. Now her work was to be reduced to overseeing a single posting, arriving at 2.00 p.m. Her wages were to be reduced slightly and she was to move to a different office.

Margaret came to her manager in tears when she heard the news. Following discussion it emerged that the issue was only partly financial. 'I've worked here for 20 years', explained Margaret, 'and I'm not going to leave just because of the money.' Margaret's problem was that she lived alone and her working routine was an important source of stability and social support. Once her manager understood the significance of the move for Margaret he jointly agreed with her to:

● Retain some of her office furniture in the move to the new office
● Look into the possibility of alternative part-time work in the mornings in a neighbouring firm.

Summary

In stage 3 you have looked at ways of exploring available routes for reaching the goals that have been selected, a specific technique—brainstorming—and an exploration of the resources available to your colleague or member of staff. You are now ready to move on to the fourth stage, which involves considering the consequences of the various possible routes.

Stage 4: Considering the consequences

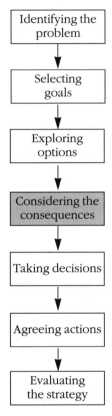

Fig. 5.9   Considering the consequences

Introduction

When you first explore alternative ways of reaching the goals that have been identified it is important not to set any preconditions or in any way evaluate the soundness of the suggested routes. But once a full range of routes has been set out it is vital to carry out a full audit of the consequences of each. So let's consider a simple but effective strategy for evaluating possible courses of problem-solving action.

Weighing up the pros and cons

The consequences of different strategies can be assessed by systematically examining the pros and cons for each one. The most straightforward way to do this is to draw up a list. Table 5.1 shows a typical format. We have included an example of a people problem—this time for a manager whose department was being disrupted by a bullying member of staff. The goal is 'Prevent the bully from disrupting my department.' The possible routes for reaching this goal are set out on the left-hand side of Table 5.1.

Table 5.1   Consequential assessment

Action	Pros	Cons
Act more aggressively	Puts bully in his place	Causes even more stress to colleagues
Act more assertively	Counters bully without putting his back up	Problem won't go away—what if I'm off sick?
Invite bully for problem-solving session	Tackles problem at source	May not work I feel vulnerable
Sack bully	Get rid of problem at a stroke	May be sued for unfair dismissal
Get a consultant in to tackle problem	Third party will have objective view Saves me spending time on problem	Costly May well put people's backs up

Unpacking the consequences

Gaining a really clear view of the pros and cons of course involves spending some time unpacking the consequences of each proposed action. This will often throw up issues that could otherwise easily be passed over. An option that involves acting in a more assertive manner may result in a task being completed on time but may have the following undesirable outcomes:

- Alienating the other person.
- The threat of sanctions for causing strife in the workplace.
- The risk of personal harm as a result of the other person's reaction.

In other words, what seems in isolation to be a viable course of action may prove in a wider context to be ill-advised.

Guarding against failure

It is vital that the process of identifying consequences is a personal one. You are inviting your colleague to consider the consequences for themselves as well as for their work and other members of staff. By keeping this focus you can guard against agreeing options that sound fine in themselves but which are unlikely to be followed through. Sacking a bully may be the best option on paper, but how likely is your colleague to do this? Consulting with staff may be the option the textbooks recommend, but perhaps your colleague has a block about this—maybe through shyness, or fear of others' reaction. Where the personal costs of an option weigh against the practical benefits you will need to decide with your colleague whether to:

- Dismiss the option because of the personal costs.
- Tackle the issue of costs, e.g. through emotional problem solving
- Risk following through the option in the expectation that the practical benefit outweighs the personal costs.

The third case may be the most expedient but longer-term problem solving will still entail tackling the more personal issues.

Additional techniques

Two techniques covered elsewhere in this book can help with the generation of a pros and cons list. You may wish to:

● Brainstorm the results of various courses of action, and the reasons for and against these (see page 116). In doing this you may uncover novel consequences, pros and cons, or options that you would otherwise have initially dismissed.
● Use visualization (see page 102). This may help your colleague to get a clearer view of the real issues that may be thrown up by a course of action. You can prompt a colleague to visualize by using simple questions such as 'What do you see happening if . . .?', and ensuring that your question is interpreted literally: you are inviting your colleague to imagine themselves into the situation.

Summary

Stage 4 has involved looking systematically at the consequences of various solution-routes. Once you have completed this review you will be in a position to help your colleague take a decision—Stage 5 in the seven-stage agenda.

Stage 5: Taking decisions

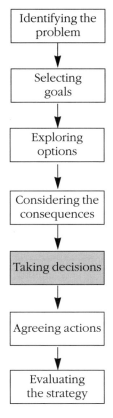

Fig. 5.10   Taking decisions

Introduction

The last stage focused on assessing the pros and cons of a range of ways of reaching problem-solving goals. Your colleague should now be in a position to choose the most feasible solution—i.e. the one that has the least negative consequences for the greatest gain. However, if this poses a problem, then this section may help you to discover what is preventing your colleague from taking a decision.

Making a solution plan

Once you have looked at the available options and their consequences your next step is to ask your colleague three questions:

1 Can their problem now be solved?
2 Do they need more information before taking a decision?
3 Which solution or package should they now pursue?

If your colleague answers 'no' to (1) and 'yes' to (2) they will need to reformulate the problem to make it solvable, or seek more information before they continue. However, if the answers are 'yes' and 'no', respectively, then a solution plan can be prepared.

Solution plans derive from the work of the psychologist D'Zurilla, on whose work we are basing this section. D'Zurilla emphasizes that any plan should aim to:

● Resolve the problem
● Maximize personal and emotional well-being
● Minimize time and effort.

Types of solution plan

Your plan may take one of two forms. A *simple plan* will emphasize a single solution or course of action. Aim to use this when one solution is likely to have a very positive outcome.

A *complex plan* can take either of two forms. It may involve either:

● Pursuing several solutions at the same time.
● Following a series of solutions: A first, and if this does not work, B; then if B does not work, C.

The first option is helpful if you decide that a battery of problem-solving techniques is most likely to succeed, when one followed in isolation would fail.

The second is valuable whenever you or your colleague is uncertain whether a particular option will succeed and you need to have others at the ready as contingency plans.

By formulating a clear plan with your colleague you can ensure that the problem is tackled in a systematic way and that you can both agree on the course to be followed. Bear in mind, too, what we have said earlier about externalization, visualization, and simplification. You can bring these to bear on your solution plan by creating a visual, shareable, clearly broken down summary of the action your colleague will now commit themselves to carrying out.

Once the plan has been prepared you will need to jointly evaluate it to ensure that it is fully workable. We will consider this further at the next stage. However, first we want to introduce one more specific type of solution plan: the 'thought form'.

Using a 'thought form'

Thought forms derive from an idea originating with the American Albert Ellis. They use the ABCDE framework to prompt your colleague to solve problems for themselves following the interview.

A thought form has been provided for you in Fig. 5.11. If you choose to use this form, you will find it useful first to introduce it to your colleague. (Fig. 5.12 illustrates one that has been completed.)

- The chances are that you will have identified several potential problems. Choose one of these, to which the person has responded emotionally in an unhelpful way, and ask them to write a summary description of it in column A.
- Then ask them to write the unhealthy emotional and behavioural response in column C.
- Briefly inference chain in column A (see p. 66).
- Next, they should note their irrational beliefs in column B.
- Ask them to note down in column D a list of possible ways in which this belief can be disputed.

Workplace problem (A)	Self-defeating thinking (B)	Emotional/ behavioural consequences (C)	Disputing self-defeating thinking (D)	New effective approach to problem (E)

Fig. 5.11 Problem-solving thought form

Workplace problem (A)	Self-defeating thinking (B)	Emotional/ behavioural consequences (C)	Disputing self-defeating thinking (D)	New effective approach to problem (E)
Giving a presentation to the Board → Giving a poor presentation to the Board	I must perform well otherwise the outcome will be awful	Anxious; inability to concentrate	*Logical:* Just because I want to perform well, how does it logically follow that I must perform well? *Empirical:* Where is the evidence that my demand must be granted? Am I being realistic? If I don't perform well, will the outcome really be awful? *Pragmatic:* Where is it getting me holding on to this belief?	Although it's strongly preferable to perform well, I don't have to There is no evidence that I will get what I demand even if it is preferable and desirable If I don't perform well, the outcome may be bad, but hardly awful and devastating! If I continue holding on to this belief, I will remain anxious and even more likely to perform badly If I change my attitude I will feel concerned and *not* anxious. Also, I'll be able to concentrate and prepare for the lecture

Fig. 5.12 A completed problem-solving thought form

● Finally, they should use column E to write up:

— New beliefs
— Healthy emotions
— Effective behaviours

Before your interview is over, make sure that your colleague understands that their emotional response is largely a result of their belief rather than the activating event.

Suggest to your colleague that they report back to you at an agreed—and not too distant—time and review the results of their thought form. Their work may have involved a greater or lesser degree of self-disclosure and you will need to allow for this. If they feel unhappy about sharing the form itself, ask them to discuss it in general terms, asking, for example:

● What did you find surprising?
● What did you find difficult?
● What did you find challenging?
● What did you find most helpful in tackling your problem?

Once the form has been used in this way you may want to suggest that it is used on a regular basis. But the form is really an aid to learning. Our experience suggests that most users are eventually able to recognize and challenge their beliefs spontaneously and dispense with the form altogether.

Summary

Stage 5 has involved deciding on possible solutions to people problems. We have explained how to use a solution plan and a thought form to assist this process, and emphasized how important it is to keep in mind the three principles of externalization, visualization, and simplification. You are now at the stage of being able to agree actions—Stage 6 in the problem-solving agenda.

Stage 6: Agreeing actions

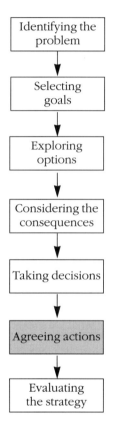

Fig. 5.13   Agreeing actions

Introduction

Your aim is now to help your colleague to take positive action to achieve their goals. We have already looked at many of the key skills involved in working at this point in the interview and here we will simply emphasize the key further points that you need to take on board.

Key issues in choosing from options

In making a final choice of strategy your aim will be to:

- Encourage your colleague to describe step by step and in detail what they intend to do.
- Focus on achievements rather than behaviour.
- Focus on a goal that will give them a genuine sense of achievement—one that will be demanding without being daunting; challenging but not overwhelming.
- Identify dividends.
- Make sure that your colleague has the resources they need to achieve the goal they have selected.

As in the previous section, let's look at each of these points in turn.

A detailed description of the intended action

We have already discussed this in relation to selecting goals (see page 109). As in any planning, positive action is likely to result only if the goal is fully specified. Here is an example of what we mean.

 CASE STUDY 5.8

Fay had met John to discuss his habitual missing of deadlines. In the course of a half-hour interview she had worked through the first five key stages of a problem-solving strategy. John had been able to recognize that his lateness was largely due to a fear that he would be a 'complete and utter failure' if anything was found to be wrong with his work. This had resulted in a tendency to prevaricate, and had on two occasions brought about the very censure that he feared. Fay had been able to help him identify negative assumptions about himself and had suggested a helpful strategy using coping imagery in association with recognition of his tendency to 'awfulize'. The interview ended like this:

Fay   Maybe you could recap on where we go from here.

John   Right. The plan is that I'll use my imagination and nous to check this habit of—what have you called it?—awfulizing.

Fay   That's it. But could you spell out what you're going to achieve as well as what you are going to do—and in a bit more detail?

John   I guess that might help, yes. Here goes. First, I'm going to pick myself up on any awfulizing—I'm going to use different words in the way we've discussed. Then I'm going to start believing in this positive picture of myself, passing you a project report on time. And I'm going to meet the deadline for the report on the Frazer network . . .

Fay   But?

John   Well, I *am* going to meet the deadline, *but* if I did just miss it by a day it would be a damn nuisance but not a disaster. It would only mean that I have some skills deficits, and it would not mean that I'm absolutely useless.

Focusing on achievements

The example has taken us into the next point on the agenda on p. 136. John began by outlining his plans simply in terms of what he was going to do. But Fay wisely reminded him of the importance of identifying tangible achievements. This, like being absolutely specific, ensures that goals are tied in to real-work tasks, and hence real concerns. It also assists subsequent evaluation—which we discuss in the next section.

Focusing on worthwhile goals

The next point on our list is closely related to the previous one. In our case study the report on the Frazer network chosen by John was in fact a relatively short piece of work. It was not a task that towered over him like a mountain. Completing the report to the deadline he had agreed with Fay would build up his confidence and enable him to go on to reach his targets on longer-term pieces of work. However, the report also demanded all his skills as a systems analyst. It was not a token piece of work—one that might have encouraged John to discount his success. (In this connection you may find it useful to refer back to page 61 where we discuss the tendency to discount the positive.)

Identifying dividends

A further source of motivation lies in identifying the dividends that improved performance will bring. We are not advocating a crude 'carrot' approach to achievement here—e.g. attempting to bribe a colleague with the promise of improved working conditions or a more interesting workload. Instead, encourage your colleague to identify for him or herself the benefits that will accrue from resolving their problem. Here, for example, is how this might have occurred in the discussion between John and Fay.

Fay   I wonder if we could just look a bit further ahead. I mean, assuming that we get this straightened out, what do you think it's going to mean for you in the longer term?

John   [*After a pause*] Well, it'll be great. I seem to have spent so much time just . . . well, just worrying. I think in the longer term I'm going to be able to get more done without working so late. What I'd really like to do is sign up for the squash club; that's something I've just not felt I've had time for.

So John's dividend was ultimately increased time for leisure. That doesn't mean to say that leisure was his motivation for working hard; but squash was a real, personal gain and importantly one that he, not Fay, was able to identify.

Checking resources are available

The final point on the list is perhaps easy to overlook, but in some respects embarking on a problem-solving strategy is like setting out on a journey. Before departing it is worthwhile checking whether the traveller has everything they need. This check can take the form of an open question, based on very wide interpretation of 'resources'. It can cover:

- *Physical resources*— e.g. office equipment including planning aids, communication aids; space and time to carry out their plan of action; a suitable health regime (see page 156–157), promoting the stamina they need to give of their best.
- *Human resources*— e.g. support staff, secretarial help, yourself to meet with and discuss progress.
- *Personal resources*—e.g. commitment to the goal; the support and understanding of colleagues; understanding of the problem-solving strategy itself.

See Figs 5.14 and 5.15 for an example of an action plan and individual task record.

Implementation

Once you have established that your colleague has all the resources they need, they can move on to implement their strategy. However, before your discussion ends make a point of:

- Discussing how they will monitor themselves.
- Agreeing a diary date for a review.

Monitoring

A simple system of self-monitoring can help ensure that a problem-solving strategy really is embarked on, and will help generate concrete data for a review. Two simple forms of self-monitoring are:

- A detailed, step-by-step action plan, with a column for recording action taken.
- A day-by-day journal recording progress towards goals.

Which you choose will depend on the nature both of the problem and the person who is tackling it, and monitoring will be most effective if the suggested procedure comes not from you but from your colleague.

Action plan

Date_ _ _ _ _ _ _ _ _ _ _ _ _ _ _

Action to be taken: _
_ _
Resources required: _
_ _
Start date: _ _ _ _ _ _ _ _ _ _ _ _ _ Review date: _ _ _ _ _ _ _ _ _ _ _ _

Action to be taken: _
_ _
Resources required: _
_ _
Start date: _ _ _ _ _ _ _ _ _ _ _ _ _ Review date: _ _ _ _ _ _ _ _ _ _ _ _

Action to be taken: _
_ _
Resources required: _
_ _
Start date: _ _ _ _ _ _ _ _ _ _ _ _ _ Review date: _ _ _ _ _ _ _ _ _ _ _ _

Action to be taken: _
_ _
Resources required: _
_ _
Start date: _ _ _ _ _ _ _ _ _ _ _ _ _ Review date: _ _ _ _ _ _ _ _ _ _ _ _

Action to be taken: _
_ _
Resources required: _
_ _
Start date: _ _ _ _ _ _ _ _ _ _ _ _ _ Review date: _ _ _ _ _ _ _ _ _ _ _ _

Fig. 5.14 Action plan

Individual task record

Name _ _ _ _ _ _ _ _ _ _ _   Date _ _ / _ _ / _ _   Negotiated with _ _ _ _ _ _ _ _

Agreed task:

The purpose(s) of the task:

What obstacles, if any, stand in your way of completing this task and how can you overcome them?

	Obstacle	**To be overcome by**
1		
2		
3		

Signed _ _ _ _ _ _ _ _ _ _ _ _ _ _ _ _ _ _

Fig. 5.15   Individual task record

Agreeing a review meeting

How and when you review will depend on the problem being tackled. If the problem is relatively simple to define and the steps involved are straight-forward, a single review after a short interval will be in order. A more complex issue, perhaps with several steps and more than one goal, may require two or more review meetings over a longer period. Your main concern, in this and other aspects of problem-solving, should be to ensure that both you and your colleague are absolutely clear about one another's:

● Roles
● Expectations
● Agreed commitments

Summary

At the end of stage 6 your colleague or staff member should be in a position to set out on a specific problem-solving strategy. In discussion with you they will have selected worthwhile goals and identified realistic ways of attaining these, and you will together have checked that they have all the resources they need for effective problem solving. However, your involvement does not end here. Once the problem has been tackled your aim should be to help your colleague evaluate the success of their strategy. This is the task of the seventh and final stage.

Stage 7: Evaluating the strategy

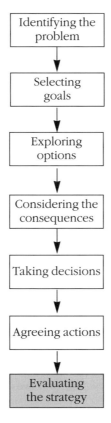

Fig. 5.16   Evaluating the strategy

Introduction

In the final stage in the problem-solving process your task is to evaluate the effectiveness of the solution your colleague has chosen. This is the one stage in the process that will, as a matter of course, take place in a separate meeting, although you could agree to carry it out by telephone if necessary. You will need to be prepared for situations in which your colleague has not attained their goals or has attained them only partially, and recognize that your own personal goal here is a 'win–win' situation in which even an apparent failure to achieve goals can be a source of valuable learning for both of you.

The review agenda

It is important to set an agenda for your evaluation session, either as the first item of business in the session itself or—preferably—before you meet. This need not be elaborate. It could cover:

● A résumé of the problem and step(s) taken to resolve it.
● A review of each step—where there is more than one.
● Future action.

Your colleague will need to have monitored their progress, as we suggested in the previous section, and you may need to remind them to bring their notes along to the meeting. Check whether they are willing to share these notes with you directly or whether they would prefer simply to refer to them when they need to.

The initial résumé of the problem can appropriately come from you, with an invitation to your colleague to comment on any points at which you may have interpreted the issue or the action differently to them.

Once you move on to the review, the initiative can pass to your colleague. This is because:

● In many respects they are the best judge of their own progress.
● Dealing with people problems is, crucially, about helping people to take responsibility for their own problems.
● Your colleague is not being examined: you are there in the first place to help rather than to critically assess.

If at the outset you have defined problem-solving action in terms of clear goals, then the review can be made in relation to each of these.

Criteria for review

There are several possible ways of reviewing. You could review the degree to which:

● The goals stated at the outset have been achieved.
● The problem stated at the outset has been resolved.

There is no need to devise a complex evaluation procedure. For example, suppose your colleague has identified several aspects of a problem, each of which they have itemized. You will probably find it sufficient to use a scale on the lines of:

achieved	some progress	unachieved
☐	☐	☐

Alternatively, you may wish to suggest to your colleague a sliding scale, itemizing the problem or goals and asking them to mark progress on a line:

Achieved _____ Unachieved

or

Resolved _____ Unresolved

Whichever method you choose, try if possible to let your colleague take the initiative, e.g. by completing the evaluation before your review meeting.

Action following the review

Here we will briefly outline three possible scenarios:

● Goals substantially achieved
● Goals partially achieved
● Goals not yet achieved

Goals substantially achieved

Where goals are wholly or substantially achieved, the problem-solving process can end. However, it may be helpful to arrange a later review when you will be able to gauge the longer-term results of the problem-solving strategy. The interval you leave will be depend on many variables, including the nature of the original problem and the confidence of your colleague that the solution is really permanent. In the meantime, and if this is in line with your business culture and your relationship with your colleague, don't be afraid to celebrate. Go out for a drink after work; buy them a present; give them a bonus; offer some more interesting or challenging work (but don't be tempted to use this as crude carrot at the start of the problem-solving process!).

Goals partially achieved

If goals have been partially achieved you will need to explore whether anything seems to be standing in the way of their full achievement. For example, your colleague may:

● Need more time.
● Need more resources or support.
● Need to try different solutions.
● Be concerned about the consequences of solving his or her problems.
● Have encountered further difficulties not explored in your previous discussion.

If more time, resources or support are required you will need to agree this and prepare a fresh, detailed action plan. This new action plan may include alternative ways of tackling the problem, in which case it may be useful to redeploy the brainstorming technique that we identified earlier, on page 116.

It may sometimes be that the prospect of a solution is itself problematic for your colleague. For example, they may have an unvoiced fear that by performing more effectively they will put themselves in line for new responsibilities that they secretly dread. Or they may resist resolving relationship difficulties because they fear the intimacy that might develop as a consequence. These and other possibilities are always worth allowing for at the review stage. But at the same time try to avoid placing these on the agenda yourself. Your aim will be to deploy the communication skills we outlined earlier in this book to enable your colleague to articulate his or her own evaluation of progress and the reason for any difficulties in reaching the goals set by him or her.

Finally, bear in mind that fresh problems may have occurred since your previous discussion. These may have the effect of subverting progress towards the goals you have agreed and may need their own problem-solving strategy— for which you may need to arrange a separate session with your colleague.

Goals unachieved

If no significant progress has been made (and what counts as significant will depend on the problem and the person), then any of the issues we have just identified may be relevant. Check also whether the goal that your colleague has agreed with you is realistic. Particularly where issues of self-acceptance are involved, an initial goal may appear too ambitious, leading to anxiety and procrastination. In this case be prepared to revise the goal, perhaps breaking it down into a series of smaller, more manageable steps.

However, absence of progress may also indicate more deep-seated problems that cannot be resolved by the problem-solving strategies we have outlined in this book. In this case you may need to suggest to your colleague that they consult outside help, e.g. a counsellor or psychotherapist. We say more about this under referral—see pages 174–176.

Summary

Completion of the seventh and final stage of the problem-solving agenda does not necessarily mean the end of problem solving. Your colleague may need to return to the agenda and tackle other problems on their list, or further issues may have developed in the meantime. However, your involvement with your colleague's problems should, if possible, take on a different dimension once the seventh stage has been reached. This will be the result of the skill-sharing process in which you need to be constantly engaged as a problem-solving manager. As a result of this process your colleague or member of staff will have learnt the seven-stage approach for themselves and will be more competent to deal with their own people problems when they arise.

References

Clarke, D. and Palmer, S. (1994) *Stress Management,* National Extension College, Cambridge.

D'Zurilla, T. J. (1986) *Problem-Solving Therapy: A Social Competence Approach to Clinical Intervention,* Springer Publishing Co., New York.

Franzen, H. and Hardaker, M. (1994) *How to Manage Managers: A Workbook for Middle Managers,* McGraw-Hill, Maidenhead.

Haley, J. (1985) *Problem-Solving Therapy: New Strategies for Effective Family Therapy,* Harper Torchbooks, New York.

O'Reilly, P. (1993) *The Skills Development Handbook for Busy Managers,* McGraw-Hill, Maidenhead.

Palmer, S. (1990) 'Stress mapping: a visual technique to aid counselling or training'. *Employee Counselling Today,* vol 2, no. 2, pp. 9–12.

Palmer, S. (1994) 'Stress management and counselling: a problem-solving approach', *Stress News,* vol. 5, no. 3, pp. 2–3.

CHAPTER 6

More skills and strategies

Introduction

In this book we have explained how to tackle people problems in relation to practical skills, thoughts, and feelings. However, when helping your staff tackle their problems appropriately you need to take into account all aspects of their personal performance: you need to consider them as a totality. We hope that this has been implied in all we have said so far. Through the astute deployment of listening and other communication skills you should be able to identify and attend to every aspect of the person with whom you are working.

But you may also find it useful to take a wider, even more systematic approach, aiming to identify all potential problem areas have been identified. One way of doing this is to use a simple inventory, covering key aspects of human personality on which people problems may have an impact.

Imagery techniques

In our experience of working with people problems, many difficulties experienced by staff in the workplace are a result of unnecessarily negative pictures of their behaviour. This applies particularly to situations where the problem is one of stress or anxiety in relation to a future work, or work-related, assignment.

There are two main types of imagery technique:

● Coping imagery
● Time projection imagery

First let's consider the simplest and most powerful imagery technique: coping imagery.

Coping imagery

  ACTIVITY 6.1

The best way to understand coping imagery is to try it out for yourself. To do this, use the following five-step activity. You will need to identify a future event about which you are anxious—either an actual forthcoming event or one that you know would be a source of anxiety were it in prospect.

So here are the five steps: we have already flagged up the first.

Step 1   Think of a future event you are anxious about.
Step 2   Note down the aspects of the event about which you are most anxious.
Step 3   Think of ways in which you can overcome these problems.
Step 4   Now visualize yourself in the situation you fear, coping with the problems you are anxious about.
Step 5   Practise this coping imagery regularly, especially every time you begin to feel anxious about the forthcoming event.

 COMMENT

Here is an example of coping imagery in practice, in the form of notes made by an employee who successfully practised the technique. This person worked as a pharmacist in an in-store pharmacy in a large supermarket.

Event

Presentation to departmental managers of the work we do in the pharmacy.

Things I feel anxious about

I was afraid I'd forget to mention important aspects of our work.

I was anxious about not being able to answer some of the questions they would ask me.

Ways in which I can overcome these problems.

I decided to:
- Make some simple notes to which I could refer.
- Ask a colleague to role play one of the other managers, asking me the sorts of question about which I felt anxious.

Visualization

I could see myself sitting at a table with the five managers. I had my notes on a pad in front of me. I felt relaxed: all the facts are there within easy visual range. I could see myself talking in a reasonably calm manner to the managers and answering their questions. If I was unable to answer a question I would tell the person that I would get them the answer after the meeting.

Practice

I made a point of repeating this visualization whenever I felt anxious in the week before the presentation was due. I found that it effectively countered the feelings that I had been experiencing. I was still a bit concerned when I stood up to speak, but I found that by reminding myself of the coping image whenever I felt 'nerves' coming on I could counter the feelings.

Contingency plans

You will see from the example we have just given that coping imagery can be used not only before the anxiety-triggering event but once the event is under way. You will need to present these to your colleague in terms of contingency plans, which they can use to cope with difficult situations. They may otherwise see your suggestion as indicating that you really believe their worst fears may be realized.

Time projection imagery

Time projection imagery is particularly helpful when a person is feeling stressed about a forthcoming event such as losing a job or ending a relationship. It aims to help put the problem in perspective. As in the previous example, we introduce the five steps involved as an activity for you to attempt yourself.

  ## ACTIVITY 6.2

Step 1   Think of a forthcoming event about which you feel stressed or anxious.

Step 2   Visualize yourself in six months time. Are you still stressed or anxious about your problem?

Step 3   Visualize yourself twelve months in the future. Will you still be as stressed? Even if you had difficulty coping with the event, can you see yourself getting on with your life?

Step 4   Visualize yourself two years from now. If you were to look back at your current problem would it still be so daunting and overwhelming? Can you see yourself acting more positively and enjoying life again? In fact, does the event still impact on your life or is it of little importance?

Step 5   Visualize yourself in five years from now. If you are unable to see a positive future, imagine pursuing a favourite task or meeting new colleagues or friends.

 ## COMMENT

Here is a typical example of time projection imagery at work.

Vince came to his boss worried about his forthcoming job loss. He had been feeling low for several days, since the news was broken to him at a staff review meeting. Here is how he used time projection imagery.

Six months' time

I'm still feeling pretty stressed. Losing my job has been a shock. I haven't found a new job and I miss the routine of the office. I feel I'm not contributing to society, and that somehow I have failed.

Twelve months' time

I don't feel quite so stressed. Life has gone on in spite of the loss of my job. I'm still bitter about the way it happened, and have bouts of low self-acceptance. But I'm starting to develop a new routine and have volunteered to help set up a new community group.

Two years from now

A lot has happened in the past year. Looking back, losing my job hasn't been quite the disaster I feared. It's been bad, yes, but not the end of the world. I had a reasonable severance payment and I can still pay the mortgage. The community work has really taken off, and the group is offering me a small honorarium for continuing as secretary. I have also managed to take a vacation with friends on the coast and put in some time landscape painting—something I never had time for when I was in my job.

Five years' time

I have adjusted to a different style of life to the one I used to have. I still miss it at times, especially the financial security. But I feel that I've been able to put back a lot into the community and have made many new friends. And with some help from my sister—a commercial artist—I have managed to develop my painting to the point where I can sell a reasonable number each year and provide an income for the occasional vacation.

Remember, this is not an account of what actually happened. This is how one employee visualized their future following the loss of their job. By giving their thoughts free rein in this way they were able to put their feelings about losing their job in perspective.

The following two case studies illustrate particular situations in which coping imagery could be appropriate. We offer these without comment and invite you to consider how the imagery might be used in each instance.

 ## CASE STUDY 6.1

Wanda worked as a seminar presenter for a small consultancy offering training to health workers. She had only recently been promoted to her post and was due to give her first seminar in a week's time. She appeared in her boss's office in the evening in a state of consternation. Wanda had worked herself into a state of great anxiety about her forthcoming presentation. She was convinced that she was going to lose track of what she wanted to say, and that she would show herself up in front of her other colleagues. Her solution to her problem was to suggest that she was not, after all, cut out for this type of work and would be better off back in the administration unit.

 ## CASE STUDY 6.2

Dave was a trainee accountant about to take his final exams. It was clear to his manager that his mind had not been on his work for some days. He had made a number of unfortunate errors in checking statistics and had also failed to detect irregularities in the business records of a new client. A problem-solving interview with his manager quickly revealed that the root of Dave's difficulties lay in his fears about his forthcoming exams. He had become obsessed with, as he put it 'dismally failing his exams'. He had recently obtained a large mortgage on the strength of his soon-to-be-acquired status as a chartered accountant and knew that any delay in gaining this new status could result in financial difficulties.

In situations of this sort, and with your colleague's compliance, you can help counter the problems by suggesting one of the imagery techniques we have described.

Managing or playing games?

Now that you have read these two accounts you may, of course, be feeling frustrated. You may feel that we are turning your managerial role into a mix of something between a therapist and a gamesmaster. You may be asking: 'If the key to coping with an event perceived as challenging is simply to put it in perspective, why, for heaven's sake, do I have to play games with my colleague? Why can't I just tell them to get it in perspective?' Our response to this is to repeat what we have said *earlier*. Telling people things rarely solves anything. Problem solving involves work, both for you and for the owner of the problem. Solutions that stick are solutions that your colleague has arrived at by their own efforts.

Stress

Whenever the problems an employee is experiencing exceed their ability to cope, stress is the result. One of the key goals you identify may therefore be to reduce stress. This is unlikely to be your only goal, since stress is itself the result of other problems, which you will need to tackle directly. However, addressing stress as a physiological phenomenon can create the conditions in which other solutions are more likely to succeed. When dealing with people problems you need to be prepared to work on all fronts!

The physiology of stress

Stress is a physiological phenomenon. When someone is in a situation they perceive as threatening or challenging, the nervous system prepares to deal with it. The heartbeat increases and blood pressure rises, while blood sugars are produced to provide extra energy. More blood goes to the heart and muscles and less to the digestive system, generating a range of long- and short-term effects. Stress manifests itself physiologically in a variety of ways. It can be useful to develop your sensitivity to these symptoms, both in yourself and in your colleagues, since they can be a clear signal of an underlying people problem that requires your intervention.

Physiological signs of stress

Be on the alert for:

- Palpitations
- Chest pain
- Indigestion
- Breathlessness
- Nausea
- Twitches
- Tiredness
- Vague aches and pains
- Skin irritations or rashes
- Increased susceptibility to allergies
- Tendency to clench fists or jaw
- Fainting
- Frequent colds, flu, or other infections
- Constipation/diarrhoea
- Rapid weight loss or gain
- Menstrual disturbances
- Asthma
- Backache or neck-ache
- Excessive sweating
- Migraines

Contrary to what some managers believe, stress is seldom positive and generally inhibits performance. What *can* enhance work performance is pressure. The precise amount of pressure needed for optimum performance varies from person to person, but it is important to be aware that too much or too little is invariably experienced as stressful. The graph in Fig. 6.1 explains this in more detail. Most of the people problems you encounter are likely to involve the right-hand curve, although you also need to be alert to problems resulting from understimulation.

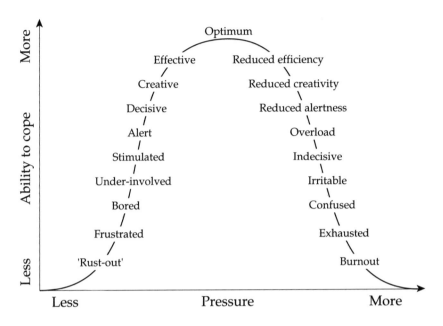

Fig. 6.1 Optimum performance curve (*Source:* Clark and Palmer, 1994)

Coping with stress

Stress is a constant theme in people problems. All the problem-solving strategies outlined in this book can have the result of reducing stress simply by enabling your colleague to cope more effectively with an overload of pressure. However, and as an important back-up, you may also want to tackle the physical effects of stress head-on. Here we outline a range of ways in which this can be done, including two specific relaxation techniques. You may find it useful to adapt this material into a handout for sharing with your colleague as part of your problem-solving strategy.

General ways of tackling the physiological effects of stress

The following factors can play a vital part in combating stress:

● *Exercise*   It's best to incorporate this into a daily routine—e.g. by walking to work or to lunch, cycling to buy a daily paper, or choosing the stairs rather than the elevator. Medics recommend a minimum of 20 minutes three times a week.

● *Nutrition*   People who eat unhealthily are less likely to be able to cope with stress—and will be physiologically disadvantaged when it comes to problem solving. High intakes of sugar, alcohol, caffeine, saturated fats, and salt can all contribute to ill health and exacerbate the effects of stress.

● *Weight*   Optimum weight minimizes health problems, including illnesses that are aggravated by stress. Diet and exercise are major influences on weight, but only 10 per cent of special diets work as people tend to relapse. The better strategy is to build a healthy diet into your lifestyle rather than go on a crash programme.

Specific strategies for tackling physiological aspects of stress

Here we outline two relaxation techniques that can help you to control stress. Like the more general ways we outlined above, these work directly on the body and can have a positive effect on the way a person feels about him or herself and on their ability to cope with adversity.

The Benson relaxation technique

This is a form of meditation based on recitation of the number one. It can be particularly helpful for controlling unwanted intrusive thoughts, which are frequently a corollary of stress.

Step 1   Find a comfortable position and sit quietly or lie down.

Step 2   Close your eyes.

Step 3   Relax your muscles in groups, starting at your face and progressing down to your toes.

Step 4   Focus on your breathing. Breath naturally through your nose. Imagine that your breathing is coming from your stomach—don't let your shoulders rise.

Step 5   In your mind, say the number one every time your breathe out.

Step 6   Continue for 5 to 20 minutes. (Here may be a good point to use coping imagery—see pages 150 to 152.)

Step 7   Finish in your own time. Keep your eyes closed for a couple of
         minutes and sit quietly.

If distracting thoughts occur during this exercise, just let them pass by and
return to repeating the number one. Don't try too hard to relax; just let
relaxation come naturally, and be prepared to make several attempts at
learning this method. If you feel uneasy at any point just open your eyes and
the feeling will pass.

Positive relaxation imagery

This technique can aid relaxation and reduce physical and emotional tension.
You will need to prepare for it by thinking of a pleasant scene to picture—
somewhere you feel relaxed. This could be real or imaginary, such as a
favourite vacation haunt, a warm bath or a country walk.

Step 1   Find a quiet place where you won't be disturbed and if possible with
         subdued lighting.
Step 2   Make yourself comfortable: sit or, if you prefer, lie down.
Step 3   Close your eyes and imagine your favourite place.
Step 4   Focus on the colours in your relaxing place.
Step 5   Now focus on one colour.
Step 6   Now focus on the sounds in your favourite place.
Step 7   Now focus on any smells or aromas.
Step 8   Now imagine touching something in your relaxing place.
Step 9   When you are ready, and in your own time, open your eyes.

Practised regularly, this technique can enable you to relax quite quickly. It can
also help if you are experiencing sleeping difficulties.

Assertion training

Helping a colleague develop assertive behaviour can enable them to tackle
situations they might otherwise shy away from, particularly those that involve
aggressive attitudes or behaviour.

You can pass on simple assertion skills to your colleague by briefing them as follows.

Explain what is meant by assertive

Contrast assertive behaviour with behaviour that is:

● Passive
● Aggressive

Someone acting *passively* tends to allow others to walk over them and gives priority to others' needs without resolving their own. Passive behaviour suggests resignation and defeatism.

Passive body language includes:

● Downcast eyes
● Shrugs
● Fidgeting
● A whining or inaudible voice

Passive language includes apologetic or 'self' words such as:

● Just
● I can't
● Forget it
● I'm sorry/afraid
● It's just me

Someone acting *aggressively* is often under the impression that they are simply being assertive. Aggressive behaviour involves angry or confrontational words and actions.

Aggressive body language involves:

● Pointing

- Shouting
- Harsh voice
- Abrupt movements of hands and arms

Aggressive language involves words and phrases such as:

- Don't be stupid!
- It's your fault
- You'd better
- For God's sake
- You must
- Come off it!

Someone acting *assertively* aims to minimize misunderstandings, avoid dominating others, or exploiting themselves. By taking a straightforward approach to situations and relationships, they defuse resentment and minimize stress.

Assertive body language includes:

- Relaxed but alert posture
- Good eye contact
- Absence of fidgeting
- Willingness to smile when praised
- Willingness to give compliments.

Assertive language includes words and phrases that are:

- *Collaborative*—Let's; we could.
- *Open*—How is it going? What do you think?
- *Owned*—I feel, I want, I hope (rather than 'one feels' or 'it's thought').

Suggest assertive rights

Offer the list of rights below as a manifesto for assertive behaviour:

I have the right to:

- Say no
- Recognize my own needs as important
- Make mistakes
- Take responsibility for what I do
- Say I don't understand
- Follow my own priorities
- Assert myself when I choose without feeling guilty
- Change my mind
- Express what I feel, in a way that respects others' rights
- Be assertive—or unassertive, without feeling guilty.

Suggest assertion techniques

There is wide range of assertion techniques—see the References for resources that cover some of these. Four of the most reliable, which you can recommend to colleagues are:

- Workable compromise
- 'Broken record'
- Fogging
- Enquiry

Workable compromise

Workable compromise can be a helpful way of minimizing confrontation. It involves one person offering the other a compromise that avoids either party suffering loss of self-respect. For example:

Manager   I'm going to need sales figures for all three departments for my meeting in the morning. Could you stay on this evening and finish collecting the data?

Clerk   I've got friends coming round for a meal tonight but I can come in early tomorrow and have the figures ready for you when you get in. Will that be all right?

Broken record

Broken record is helpful when someone needs to reiterate their own viewpoint in the face of challenge. It involves calmly reiterating a position without becoming involved in an irrelevant argument.

Clerk   I need to use the copier now, I've been waiting for ten minutes and that's long enough.

Secretary My boss says this job has to take priority over everything else in the department.

Clerk   So you couldn't care less about my lunch break or the way my own work will be messed up. I need to use it now, come on.

Secretary I've been asked to give this job priority. All the other work will have to wait.

Clerk   Look, I've got other work too, it's important and I don't give a damn about your priorities.

Secretary The job I'm doing is the most pressing one, and my boss says everything else will have to be done after it.

Fogging

Fogging is helpful when someone is faced with a blanket criticism. The technique involves acknowledging whatever elements are justified in a way that maintains the self-respect of the person being targeted.

Here is an example:

Supervisor I'm fed up with your work. You never check your typing and customers are always ringing to complain about mistakes in your letters.

Supervisee I did send out three letters without checking them last week and two people remarked on errors. I take full responsibility for those.

Enquiry

Enquiry involves asking for constructive feedback when the immediate reaction might be to react in a confrontational way. This both clarifies the nature of the accusation and helps defuse the anger behind it. An example might be:

Manager   You're completely hopeless as a salesperson.

Salesperson   In what way do you find me hopeless?

Time management

An employee experiencing stress can help minimize this by managing their time more effectively. This can be particularly helpful if the management involves allocating more time to social activities and relaxation. You can help a colleague by selecting from a wide range of time-management techniques; but bear in mind that the choice needs to be theirs. Here we give a summary of tried and tested approaches. For a wider range refer to the resources in the references section pp. 197–202.

At the end of each day, list your priority tasks for day following.

- Finish one task before starting on the next.
- Allow time for the unexpected.
- Do one task at a time.
- If a task seems daunting, divide it into smaller ones.
- Use your assertion skills to say 'no' where necessary.
- Prepare for meetings by listing items you want to discuss.
- Batch outgoing telephone calls and list points you want to cover in the call.
- Use a timer to monitor the time you spend on the phone.
- Open and deal with incoming mail at the same time, so that you handle it only once.
- Do difficult tasks first, rather than put them off.
- Obtain and provide detailed instructions. If in doubt, ask.
- Schedule regular breaks into your day.

Keeping a time log

If a colleague finds it hard to pin down their time-management problems, suggest that they keep a log of the way in which they use their time. This can be done four or five times a day at regular intervals, over the course of a week, noting down:

● How time has been spent
● What interruptions occurred
● Any other factors that intervened to prevent work being completed.

You can then review the log in discussion with your colleague and identify helps and hindrances to managing their time. The hindrances can then be tackled as either:

● Problems which can be eliminated.
● Problems which need to be allowed for and scheduled in when making further plans.

The BASIC ID

The inventory that follows has been adapted from that constructed by the psychologist Arnold Lazarus. It uses the initials BASIC ID to cover the following aspects of human performance.

B behaviour—what the person is doing or avoiding
A affect—in other words, feelings, emotions
S sensation—bodily processes
I imagery—the mental pictures that are being experienced
C cognition—what the person is thinking
I interpersonal—relationships with other people
D drugs, biology—factors affecting physical functioning.

People problems at work may impact on any or all of these areas, and much is to be gained from keeping these in mind when working with your staff to tackle difficult issues.

Table 6.1 expands on the above list with some typical examples of resulting problems.

Table 6.1   BASIC ID assessment

Aspect		Example of impact on person
B	behaviour	Avoiding colleagues
A	affect (emotion)	Irritability, anxiety, guilt
S	sensation	Tension, headaches
I	imagery	Seeing self as being humiliated; bad dreams
C	cognition	Self-damning beliefs (e.g. I am a useless accountant)
I	interpersonal	Loneliness
D	drugs, biology	Heavy smoking; lack of exercise

You can use the BASIC ID in a variety of ways. For example, you could:

● Explain it to your colleague and suggest they use it as the basis for their own problem audit, either on the spot or in a subsequent discussion.
● Explain it to a colleague but take the lead yourself in working through the inventory.
● Keep it at the back of your mind as a simple *aide-mémoire* as you work with your colleague.
● Use it for your own self-audit.

Or indeed, in any way you find useful. However, it is vital not to use the BASIC ID as a way of cross-examining a member of staff. This will almost certainly be counter-productive, and at worst give the impression of a set of standards which they may either pass or fail. Let's consider this a little further.

Reviewing the BASIC ID

Suppose you are using the inventory at an exploratory stage in discussions with a member of staff. Your aim will be to ensure that all aspects in which there may be difficulties have been fully explored. You will be aware that behind the presenting problem there may well be a series of further ones, more or less closely related to it. As discussion proceeds, you may find it useful to cover the BASIC ID in a series of simple interventions such as those given in Table 6.2.

Table 6.2 BASIC ID assessment questions

Question	Aspect	
Are you avoiding anything or anybody?	B	behaviour
How do you feel when that happens?	A	affect
Do you just think that or do you feel it in your body somehow?	S	sensation
How do you imagine yourself reacting?	I	imagery
What do you say to yourself when that happens?	C	cognition
What about your social life; how's that going?	I	interpersonal
What sort of exercise are you getting these days?	D	drugs, biology

We are not suggesting that you use just the questions given in Table 6.2. There are dozens of ways in which you can raise issues of BASIC ID, and equally many ways in which these issues may present themselves to you. But developing your skills and awareness in this area will help to ensure that all aspects of a people problem are explored at as early a stage as possible. It will then be your task to work with your colleague to identify an appropriate way of tackling the problem, in the way we have discussed earlier in this book.

Table 6.3 Individual training programme

Aspect	Could be tackled by
Behaviour	Step-by-step response to challenges
Affect	A training programme (for example, in anger management)
Sensation	Relaxation techniques (for example, tapes, yoga classes)
Imagery	Countering negative images with positive ones
Cognition	Rehearsing positive statements
Interpersonal	Developing more social contacts
Drugs, biology	Taking time to exercise

Acting on the BASIC ID

The inventory we have outlined will help you pinpoint problems that vary greatly in their seriousness. Some—perhaps the majority—can be dealt with in the ways we have discussed in this book. Table 6.3 on p. 168 outlines some typical ways in which problems identified by the BASIC ID could be tackled.

However, it is vital to be on the alert for the need to offer more specialist support where necessary. Essentially, in the workplace the BASIC ID is most useful as an aide-mémoire or for a good self-audit when you are focusing on, or dealing with, your own problems.

References

Back, K., Back, K. and Bates, T. (1991) *Assertiveness at Work: A Practical Guide to Handling Awkward Situations,* McGraw-Hill, Maidenhead.

Benson, H. (1976) *The Relaxation Response,* Collins, London.

Clarke, D. and Palmer, S. (1994) *Stress Management,* National Extension College, Cambridge.

Hauck, P. (1980) *Calm Down,* Sheldon Press, London.

Hauck, P. (1981) *How to Stand Up for Yourself,* Sheldon Press, London.

Lazarus, A. A. (1977) 'Toward an egoless state of being', in A. Ellis and R. Grieger (eds), *Handbook of Rational-Emotive Therapy,* McGraw-Hill, New York, United States of America.

Lazarus, A. A. (1984) *In the Mind's Eye,* Guilford Press, New York, New York, United States of America.

Lazarus, A. A. (1989) *The Practice of Multimodal Therapy,* Johns Hopkins University Press, Baltimore, Maryland, New York, United States of America.

Palmer, S. and Dryden, W. (1991) 'A multimodal approach to stress management', *Stress News,* vol. 3, no. 1, pp. 2–10.

Palmer, S. and Dryden, W. (1995) *Counselling for Stress Problems,* Sage, London.

Palmer, S. and Strickland, L. (1995) *Stress Management: A Quick Guide,* Folens, Dunstable.

CHAPTER 7

Wider issues

Recognizing your boundaries

In the previous section we explained in some detail what dealing with people problems involves, and what it does not involve. We wanted to dispel any notion that you need to be either an all-powerful mister fixit, or a workplace shrink. We have also explained the sorts of problem with which you might need to deal as a manager, or simply as a colleague. Now we want to put these two points together and consider the likely boundaries to your competence as a workplace problem-solver. At what point will you need to point your colleague towards other sources of help and support? In other words, when will you need to *refer*?

 ACTIVITY 7.1

On the next page you'll find a quick review to get you started. Below we list the main sorts of people problem from outside the workplace that are likely to impact on job performance and morale. Rate them as follows according to how important you think it would be to refer the member of staff to other sources of help:

***   very important
**   important
*   fairly important

Don't hesitate too long over these—this is just an initial check, not an in-depth analysis. Your ratings will be a rough guide only and will vary according to the nature of the problem.

Problem

- Relationships with partner or spouse
- Relations with children
- Relations with other family members
- Finance
- Housing
- Legal issues
- Social isolation
- Use of alcohol and drugs
- Psychiatric help
- Physical health
- Sexual adjustment
- Bereavement and impending loss

 COMMENT

Below we give our ratings for the same issues. If your views differ significantly from these, you may need to think again about your competence. Alternatively, you may have had specialist training and be very well able to tackle the problem-type in question.

More is said about each issue in the referral section on page 174–176. They are included here to give you an overview of the wide range of people problems you as a manager can expect to encounter.

A checklist of people problems	Referral rating
Relationships with partner or spouse	**
Relations with children	***
Relations with other family members	**
Finance	*
Housing	*
Legal issues	*
Social isolation	**
Use of alcohol and drugs	***
Psychiatric help	***
Physical health	**
Sexual adjustment	**
Bereavement and impending loss	*

So to repeat, you will also need to be willing to recognize the boundaries of your own competence to deal with problems. This book is not about becoming a workplace counsellor, and you will need to be prepared to refer colleagues for appropriate, independent help where necessary.

Of course, it may not always be immediately apparent that such help really is needed. A problem that initially presents itself to you as one within your competence to deal with may mask other more or less serious ones which are beyond your capability. This tension between *presenting* and *actual* leads to the first of three key principles we want to introduce for dealing with people problems.

Developing an organizational problem-solving strategy

Creating a problem-reducing environment

Earlier in this book we drew your attention to the value of drawing attention to the support that staff can gain from stability zones and rituals. You can maximize this support by creating workplace stability zones in which staff can unwind, relax, socialize, or take their mind off the job. Some organizations have set up gymnasiums where staff can keep fit, or relaxation classes to help employees combat stress. These facilities do not necessarily remove sources of stress, but they do enhance the ability of staff to cope with it.

Referral

We have already introduced the idea of referral. We now want to offer some further suggestions based on the work you have done and the experience you have gained since then.

When you refer a colleague elsewhere for help, it is vital to find out about their expectations. These have been shown to have a significant impact on the success of therapy, and they are far more important than any particular enthusiasm of your own. For example, someone whose problem is an eating disorder may have become excited about a recent television documentary about the potential of hypnotism in treating it. You may feel a considerable amount of personal scepticism about this. But the reality is that any potential therapy has been given a head start by your colleague's positive attitude.

Here is checklist of points to ascertain before referring a colleague for outside help.

Helpers' checklist

- What if any previous outside help have they received?
- For any such help, how do you rate it?
- Whether or not you have been helped in the past, what approach do you feel is most likely to help you with your problem?
- With what sort of person would you feel most at ease, e.g. in terms of:
    – gender
    – ethnicity
    – age
    – therapeutic approach

You may need to explain the last point at greater length, with due regard to your colleague's level of understanding. A simple way of explaining therapeutic approaches is in terms of the following three-way division:

- Person-centred/humanistic
- Cognitive-behavioural
- Psychodynamic

It may be that your colleague will understand these distinctions, and will simply be able to indicate which approach they feel most at ease with; or they may be able to identify a source of help for themselves. However, the chances are that they will not be familiar with the range of therapeutic possibilities, in which case you will need to translate the options into terms they understand. Some possible ways of phrasing your enquiry are as follows—but ultimately you will need to match what you say more precisely to the level of understanding and personal language of your colleague.

Person-centred/humanistic

Would you feel at ease with a therapist who:

- Sees as their main aim creating a helpful and empathetic environment in which you can work through your own problems?

Cognitive-behavioural

Would you feel at ease with a therapist who:

- suggests practical ways in which you can tackle specific problems? (This approach is similar to the one we have described in this book.)

Psychodynamic

Would you feel at ease with a therapist who:

- helps you to explore the impact of your past on your current problems?

Referring appropriately

Below we repeat in more detail the checklist of people problems we compiled at the start of this section, with the opportunity for you to add your own details of sources of outside help. On page 197–202 we include a list of organizations who may be able to help employees with a variety of problems or training needs.

A checklist of people problems, with referral rating

Relationships with partner or spouse **
Remarks
Your own contacts
Phone   e-mail

Relations with children ***
Remarks
Your own contacts
Phone   e-mail

Relations with other family members **
Remarks
Your own contacts
Phone   e-mail

Finance *
Remarks
Your own contacts
Phone   e-mail

Housing *
Remarks
Your own contacts
Phone   e-mail

Legal issues *
Remarks
Your own contacts
Phone   e-mail

Social isolation **
Remarks
Your own contacts
Phone   e-mail

Use of alcohol and drugs ***
Remarks
Your own contacts
Phone   e-mail

Psychiatric help ***
Remarks
Your own contacts
Phone   e-mail

Physical health **
Remarks
Your own contacts
Phone   e-mail

Sexual adjustment **
Remarks
Your own contacts
Phone   e-mail

Bereavement and impending loss *
Remarks
Your own contacts
Phone   e-mail

Yourself as a person problem

Most of this book has focused on other people as problems. Here we want to briefly remind you of some of the problems you yourself may experience in your role as a problem-solving manager.

When your own feelings interfere

Check back to the case study of Gerry and Kieran on page 34 to 35. There we explored a block to problem solving that arose as a result of an experience on the part of Gerry that was analogous to one of yours. Blocks may also come about because the other person has different values to ourselves.

 ACTIVITY 7.2

To get to grips with this important point, pause for a moment to think how an encounter similar to that between Gerry and Kieran might have encountered the issue of different value systems.

 COMMENT

Any number of responses are possible. Here are two:

Gerry might have been a Catholic; Kieran might have been requesting more time to look after his wife following an abortion.

Gerry might have been a committed trade unionist. Kieran might have wanted to spend time at home to enable his wife to campaign for a right-wing political party.

In both of these cases, Gerry faces the challenge of setting aside, but not abandoning, his own beliefs, and the feelings that are linked to them, in order to respond fairly to Kieran's request.

To end this section, we suggest you carry out the following review activity, which will help develop your own awareness of potential barriers in your relationships with colleagues.

 ACTIVITY 7.3

This activity is designed to help you become aware of your nightmare colleague. Build up a profile of the person you would find it least easy to accept in a disinterested way by completing the list below:

Age:

Ethnic origin:

Sexual orientation:

Religious beliefs:

Political beliefs:

Pastimes:

Dress:

Now consider what positive steps you could take to enable you to work more effectively with your 'nightmare colleague'. Write a list of possible helpful interventions and strategies.

When your own thoughts interfere

Just as there is always a danger that your own feelings may draw your attention away from the other person, so your own thoughts may get in the way of fully attending to what they are saying. This may be a particular issue in the early stages of practising a problem-solving approach. Having gained a clear intellectual grasp of the solution-focused agenda, you may feel the need to remind yourself of this as the other person explains their problem. This may impact on you in three specific ways.

Parallel thoughts

You may find that you are focusing both on what the person is saying and on your own thoughts. If so, don't be fooled into thinking that you are listening properly. The chances are that at best you are listening to what is being said at only one level, and are missing important hints or nuances. On the other hand, try not to become over-anxious. Recognize your parallel thoughts for what they are and respectfully lay them on one side. You may find it helpful to use an image to help you do this. For example, you could picture a padlocked chest with your thoughts inside.

Splitting off

You may lapse into your own internal dialogue and entirely lose touch with what the other person is saying.

If this happens, don't panic. Again the best course is to be honest. Be honest with the person who is talking to you. Ask them to pause and explain what has happened. Be honest with yourself and ask why this has happened. Perhaps the cause is mainly physiological—you are at the end of tiring day. Or perhaps there is something about the person or the problem which prompts in you the urge to escape. Or maybe it is a boring problem. The second instance may be a signal that you are reaching the limits of your own competence as a problem-solver and that you need to refer the person elsewhere. Alternatively, simply recognizing that you are splitting off may draw your attention back.

Anticipation

You may feel you know exactly what the other person is about to say and either:

● Finish their sentence for them.

or

● Respond before they have finished speaking.

Anticipation is usually a sign of impatience, or insecurity, or both. If you really do feel the pressure of other commitments in a problem-solving interview, you can:

- *In the short term:* explain that you are finding it hard to concentrate on the problem and fix a time when you know you will be able to give it your fuller attention.
- *In the medium term:* reflect on whether there was something in what the other person was saying that you felt uneasy about. If so, recognition may in itself be sufficient, as with parallel thoughts; or you may want to refer them on to a colleague or a source of outside help.
- *In the long-term:* review your priorities. Perhaps you are finding it difficult to make time for people. But economy in dealing with people problems is often a false economy. Without a solution they will keep returning, and take up even more of your time.

A problem-solving environment

A problem-solving discussion works best if carried out in an environment where you and colleague both feel at ease. Use the following checklist to ensure that you have a suitable place for meeting.

Do you have a place where you and your colleague will be:

	Yes	No
● Free from interruptions?	☐	☐
● Able to speak without being overheard?	☐	☐
● At ease?	☐	☐
● Comfortable?	☐	☐
● Hearable without having to raise your voices?	☐	☐

If you answered 'no' to any of these questions you should make arrangements now to make good the deficit; otherwise you may find that your problem-solving skills are undermined by an unsympathetic environment.

Putting yourselves at ease

We have used the plural here to emphasize the importance of both your colleague and yourself being at ease during a problem-solving discussion.

Timing

Making time

It's unlikely that you'll be able to have the most constructive discussion if you are pressed for time. The way in which you make time will depend on three factors:

● The nature of the presenting problem
● Your colleague's availability
● Your own availability

The mix of these factors will determine whether you:

● Meet them there and then—as soon as your colleague presents the problem.
● Arrange to meet them a short time afterwards—say, later that day if they speak with you in the morning.
● Arrange to meet them after a longer interval.

The second option is likely to be the most attractive one in many circumstances. That way you have the chance to reflect on the situation and the strategies with which you can tackle it, and your colleague has the chance to prepare for the discussion. A short postponement has other advantages, too:

● It will help you to ensure that you can clear some time to speak without being interrupted. (However, in an emergency be prepared for a complete shut-down of systems to tackle a pressing problem. This should be within the competence of any manager: witness the speed with which heads of state reprioritize their business to attend to crisis!)

● It will enable you to check whether you feel ready to tackle this particular problem. We emphasize on page 171 the importance of referral to an outside consultant, and it's as well to keep this option in mind right from the start. If you sense that you are maybe not the most suitable person for your colleague to consult, be ready to air this at the start of the interview and, if your hunch is confirmed, be ready to suggest an alternative source of problem-solving support.

 ## CASE STUDY 7.1

Ray went into the washroom one morning and heard sobs coming from one of the cubicles. In response to his 'You OK in there?' Zak emerged looking shaken and red-eyed. He explained what Ray had already half-guessed, that his partner had just died of AIDS after a short but painful illness. 'Could I speak with you in private somewhere, Ray?' asked Zak. Ray arranged to meet him in his office later in the morning. In the meantime he reflected that his 23-year-old son had recently been diagnosed HIV-positive and that he and his wife were very upset by the situation. Maybe he wasn't the best person for Zak to speak with. As a result Ray had a short meeting with Zak, for which he was able to prepare both physically (ensuring his secretary would field phone calls) and psychologically (reminding himself that counselling was not on the agenda, in view of his own skills and the nature of the problem). Ray made it clear that he could help with arrangements for leave, but referred Zak on to a colleague in personnel who had trained as a counsellor and would be better able to help Zak through his distress.

Managing time

Once you have made time, you need to manage time effectively in the interview. Key points to bear in mind are as follows:

● Make clear at the start how much time is available for the interview, and explain to your colleague that for that duration you won't be interrupted. You will need to use your skill as a manager to set aside a period that is neither so short as to hurry your colleague, nor so long as to leave them daunted. Within reason, most of us pace what we have to say according to the time available, and as much ground can be covered in 15 minutes as 50 in the right environment.

● Avoid repeatedly checking your watch. This can be very offputting to many people, particularly if they are feeling vulnerable and alert to any sign that their problem is boring or inconsequential. Check that there is a clock at which you can glance momentarily and without any bodily movement. Alternatively, you could signal to your colleague at the start that you will need to check the time at intervals, minimizing the chances of their interpreting this in a negative way.

● You may find it useful to indicate to your colleague that you have only, say, five or ten minutes left. This gives you both the chance to ensure that you have covered all the intended ground during your discussion.

Managing space

We have already emphasized the importance of a suitable environment. What this means in practice will depend partly on the particular culture prevailing in your workplace. However, here are some general guidelines for managing space.

Lighting

Try to avoid sitting with the light behind you. This can intensify feelings of being 'in the spotlight' for some people, and leave them ill at ease. Equally, over-subdued lighting can give the wrong signals: problem solving requires you both to be as alert and aware as possible.

Furnishings

There are no hard and fast rules about furnishings, but try to ensure that you are both able to feel relaxed and comfortable. Beware of trying to organize your office like a consulting room. A therapist might advise against any barrier—such as a desk—between yourself and your colleague. But in a work situation, with a focus on tasks and job roles, an employee may feel exposed if nothing interposes between you.

Similarly, keep in mind the usefulness of office equipment. If you have a whiteboard in your office, you may find it helpful to use it for drawing up checklists or maps of problems (but be sure to erase it after your meeting). Overhead projectors, flipcharts, laptops and even pocket calculators can all play their part. Remember, you are not a therapist.

Position

Think carefully about position before your problem-solving encounter. A small barrier can be a positive help—and provides a surface to make notes on! However, conducting a problem-solving interview from one side of a large desk or table is unlikely to be satisfactory, since it tends to emphasize confrontation rather than collaboration. Sitting directly opposite your colleague without intervening furniture may also be experienced as inhibiting. Instead, try if possible to sit at an angle to them of around 140°—somewhere between head-on and side-by-side. Be aware, too, of the effects of distance. These vary according to culture. For example, a white male British manager probably needs to be about 1–1.5m from his colleague: closer and they may experience him as intrusive; further and they may interpret him as psychologically distant, too. On the other hand, an Italian or Mexican might find greater closeness appropriate.

Posture

Much has been written about body language, not all of it backed up by sound research. Contrary to some writers, we would not claim that posture and expression offer an infallible insight into the true thoughts and feelings of the person with whom you are conversing. However, it's important to be aware of the reassurance that you can convey by an open posture.

Try to keep your hands and limbs relaxed, your arms unfolded and your face unshielded. If possible, lean very slightly towards your colleague, as you would in a normal conversation. Resist any tendency to avoid eye contact, but beware of making self-conscious use of such contact—with the risk of this being interpreted as staring.

Finally, be alert for any physical signs of tension or defensiveness in your colleague—signals to you to tread carefully as you help them explore and then tackle their problem.

Decor

The type of decor that is suitable for a problem-solving environment depends largely on your particular working culture. However, it is important to be alert to any potential difficulties your working space may raise for your colleague.

 CASE STUDY 7.2

A middle manager in a small engineering firm met an employee whose work was suffering as a result of worries generated by his divorce. Although the manager was able to confidently use problem-solving skills, he found his employee very defensive and the discussion was inconclusive. He later found from a third party that he had inhibited conversation by leaving out on his desk his wife's recent Valentine card and pictures of his young family. The employee had seen the card and pictures as 'rubbing salt in the wound' (as he put it).

Summary

Creating a problem-solving environment requires care. Ideally you will need to find space that is quiet and confidential. On the other hand your colleague may be intimidated by somewhere that seems too obviously like a consulting room—somewhere staff go when they are in some sort of trouble. Aim for an environment that is a mixture of familiar, relaxing, and confidential.

Finally, however, be flexible. If your colleague would clearly be happiest talking things over during lunch in a snack bar, or on a park bench, try to arrange this. A car journey might prove an ideal time for a problem-solving session. But if a colleague approaches you in an elevator with a problem, listen to them there and then if necessary. Be prepared to solve problems on the hoof, be pragmatic. The approach we suggest in this book can be applied in any situation and if you wait for the perfect problem-solving moment in the perfect location, the chances are the problem will have taken its toll—resignation, job loss, or long-term disruption of relationships and the work environment.

Organizational issues

The problem-solving approach we have identified in this book has implications for the overall culture of organizations, and—in larger organizations—for particular departmental subcultures. The more these implications are taken on board the more effective the problem-solving strategies are likely to be. Conversely, if you, as a manager intent on dealing with people problems, are working in a climate at odds with your approach, your individual ability to help your colleagues is likely to be impaired.

Organizational cultures

Four principle types of organizational culture have been identified:

- Power culture
- Role culture
- Task culture
- Person culture

These can be characterized briefly as follows.

Power culture

The organization takes an aggressive stance towards competitors, which is reflected in working relationships. Great importance is attached to the balance of interests and resources, sometimes at the expense of the task in hand, and individuals tend to be seen as motivated by self-interest.

Role culture

The organization values stability and takes a cautious attitude to change. Decisions are made following set procedures and individual employees tend to be concerned with status and legitimacy. Adaptation to changing market conditions may be slow as a result, though the organization may thrive in a stable business environment.

Task culture

The organization is concerned to accomplish the task in hand, and is likely to value rules and procedures only in so far as they help this. People are valued for what they can do rather than for the nominal status of their role and, internally, collaboration is valued above competition.

Person culture

The organization sees an individual primarily as a tool for personal development. As a result, tasks tend to be allocated according to personal need rather than organizational imperatives. Decisions tend to rely on reaching consensus—even if this delays reaching a conclusion.

Strengths and weaknesses of cultures

Each of the four cultures has its characteristic strengths and weaknesses, and there is no recipe for a totally effective organization. This is partly because the prevailing culture needs to reflect changing external environments: what is appropriate at one time may not be appropriate at another. In addition, even moderately small organizations are likely to harbour a variety of different cultures, making the prevailing overall culture difficult to characterize.

A business where managers successfully deal with people problems in the way described in this book is therefore likely to contain elements from all of these cultures. However, it is also clear that the characteristics most favourable to the problem-solving approach are found in task and person cultures. These characteristics are sufficiently clear to enable us to speak of a 'problem-solving culture'. Let's look at what this might mean in practice.

A problem-solving culture

An organization that maximizes an individual's potential to deal with people problems is likely to have the following characteristics.

Autonomy

● Elements from: person culture, task culture

An organization in which individual managers are given as much autonomy as possible in the day-to-day running of their department is likely to be more amenable to dealing with people problems than one in which a high degree of administrative control is exercised.

The principle of subsidiarity is highly relevant here. This asserts that: 'No function that can effectively be carried out by an organizational sub-unit should be performed by a larger unit.'

Applied to your own situation as a problem-solving manager, this means that your organization needs to be able to recognize:

● Your individual competence to deal with people problems.
● Your colleagues' potential for dealing with their own problems, which you, as a manager, can help them to realize.

If you work in an organization that either sees people problems as blameworthy, or defines your own managerial role too narrowly—not valuing time spent dealing with people problems—you are unlikely to be able to fully implement the ideas outlined in this book.

Flexibility

● Elements from: task culture

In order to deal effectively with people problems you will need to be able to work flexibly. Although some problems can be anticipated, very many occur out of the blue and require prompt action. If you are part of a culture that sees departure from a rigid daily routine as a shortcoming, you are unlikely to be able to function well as a problem-solving manager.

Inverted hierarchies

● Elements from: task culture, person culture

In an innovative organization, ideas are likely to flow in all directions, not just from the top down. This results in an inverted hierarchy. If you, as a manager, have purchased and been inspired by the ideas in this book, then you will want to see your problem-solving approach implemented not just in your own section but throughout your organization. Otherwise the consequences are likely to be that:

● Your own approach will be seen as a threat by colleagues, who see the positive results of your problem-solving style but are unwilling to learn more about it—in other words, learning from subordinates or other departments raises issues of status
● Staff moving to other parts of the organization are likely to experience renewed stress as they react against a less enabling management style.

Trust and openness

● Elements from: person culture

Organizations thrive when they value and trust their employees as people in their own right. In a climate of trust and openness, staff develop genuine loyalty. When necessary they are prepared to commit additional time and energy to achieving organizational goals, since these goals are part of their own, personal horizon, not just a distant corporate one. Furthermore, by being involved personally in the organization they are willing to give more of themselves in return. As a result, their thinking will be less constrained by a narrow interpretation of their role, and they are more likely to contribute to innovation.

Your approach to dealing with people problems at work will:

● Help your colleagues to feel that they are valued as people in their own right, whose problems will be sensitively dealt with rather than brushed aside as a shortcoming.
● Foster a positive—and productive—sense of trust and openness. We have emphasized throughout that your goal as a problem-solving manager is to enable your colleagues to tackle their own problems more effectively, by being as open as possible about your problem-solving strategy. We have

also emphasized the value of trusting your colleagues to develop their own problem-solving potential.

● Help your colleagues reach their full potential.

Collaboration not competition

● Elements from: person culture; task culture

All successful organizations need to be competitive. However, the dynamism required to compete can be best generated by an internal culture of collaboration, with a strong sense of shared goals. Individuals working as part of a team are likely to be more willing to:

● Recognize problems in themselves.
● Admit to problems when they recognize them.
● Proffer help to colleagues experiencing problems.
● Accept help from colleagues when this is offered.

In a competitive work environment, individual problems tend to be suppressed for as long as possible. This may be an apparent short-term gain, but it rarely compensates for the loss in terms of reduced working effectiveness and, ultimately, sickness and absenteeism.

Willingness to learn

● Elements from: task culture

This is the final organizational characteristic in our list but it is arguably the most significant. An organization that deals effectively with people problems needs to take a positive approach to these problems. In particular it needs to:

● Encourage its managers to develop their problem-solving skills
● Approach problems as opportunities for learning rather than as shortcomings.

Let's briefly look at each of these points.

Skills development

If you have tackled this book with the encouragement of your organization the chances are that it also takes seriously the value of problem-solving skills development. If you are reading it on your own initiative, that's fine for you . . . but your skills will stand the best chance of developing if your organization is behind you and takes seriously the learning needs of its managers. Organizations that succeed in the next century will be learning organizations; they will see learning not as a once for all activity that ends at the age of twenty or so but as something that continues throughout life. Support for employees learning new skills, at whatever level in the organization, will be a high priority.

Opportunities not shortcomings

People problems can be viewed in two ways:

● As occasions to criticize someone's performance, and perhaps mark them down as unsuitable for promotion
● As opportunities for learning, so that the person and the organization as a whole can perform more effectively in the future.

This book has taken the second line. We believe that people problems are rarely simply a result of one individual's shortcomings. The corollary of this is that dealing with these can be an opportunity for organizational and individual growth, and that an organization that takes seriously these opportunities will be able to attract and retain employees more effectively.

Summary

You may not, of course, be in a position to influence the overall culture of your organization. If this is the case, you may need to work in an environment that is at odds with your own approach. However, even organizations that at the outset have been reluctant to recognize the impact of people problems on performance have been rapidly convinced of the value of taking them seriously—and this in turn has encouraged a cultural shift. All the signs are that the organizations that succeed in the next century will be those that care for the whole employee.

A final list of dos and don'ts

As we have emphasized, this book is not intended to make you into a workplace counsellor or therapist. Our intention throughout has been simply to explain a series of straightforward strategies to help with people problems at work. To underline this, on p. 193 is a final summary of dos and don'ts to bear in mind when dealing with people problems at work.

References

Culley, S. (1991) *Integrative Counselling Skills in Action,* Sage, London.

Dixon, N. (1994) *The Organizational Learning Cycle: How We Can Learn Collectively,* McGraw-Hill, Maidenhead.

WIDER ISSUES ■

Don't	Do
Assume that if a colleague is late, or makes mistakes, or seems accident prone, that there must be a deeper explanation for this.	Allow for the cock-up interpretation of human behaviour as well as the conspiracy one.
Assume that you have the key to resolving their problems.	Nurture your colleague's own ability to explore, define, and resolve their problems.
Deny as bad something that your colleagues feels is bad.	Help your colleague to acknowledge that just because something is bad, it needn't be 'horrible'.
Use silence as a form of intimidation.	Accept that people sometimes just want to say nothing, and at other times welcome an invitation to say more.
Withhold simple information if it seems appropriate to pass this on.	Pass on relevant information if your colleague could use, or is requesting, this.
Be tempted to tell your colleague what to do.	Invite your colleague to suggest a possible problem-solving strategy.
Assume that you can 'know how the other person feels'.	Be tentative in your conclusions about others' feelings and experience.
Assume that because you seem to have experienced and solved a similar problem, then you can pass on to your colleague a short cut to solving their own.	Encourage your colleague to devise their own problem-solving strategies.
Be tempted to talk about yourself; particularly, don't be drawn into offering anecdotes.	Offer information about yourself if your colleague requests it—particularly if they need information about your own immediate thoughts or feelings.
Try to force the pace of your interview.	Work at your colleague's pace—while recognizing the need to move on to other workplace tasks.
Assume there can be a truly satisfactory solution to any problem.	Be willing to accept a solution that is 'good enough' for present purposes.
Assume that because someone has a personal problem, that it originated in their childhood.	Be open to your colleague's own understanding of the cause of their problem.
Assume that because a problem originated at an earlier phase in a someone's life, they can only tackle it by reliving their past.	Help your colleague to clarify and adjust their beliefs about how a problem has originated and how they can now best tackle it.
Be tempted to see yourself as a guru.	Accept that you and your colleague are both learning, together.
Assume that what you regard as a successful outcome is the same as what your colleague assumes is a successful outcome.	Invite your colleague to comment on what makes for a successful outcome.

Now that you've read this book, the authors would be interested to hear your views and experience of their problem-management approach. Please write to them:

Centre for Stress Management
156 Westcombe Hill
London SE3 7DH
UK

Further resources

Here are the contact details of people and organizations who can provide further training, materials and information for managers on dealing with people problems at work.

Organizations

United Kingdom

Association for Counselling at Work
Eastlands Court
St Peter's Road
Rugby
Warks CV21 3QP

British Association for Cognitive and Behavioural Therapists
23 Partridge Drive
Baxenden
Accrington
Lancs RB5 2RL

tel. 0161 724 6321

British Association for Counselling
1 Regent Place
Rugby
Warks CV21 2JP

tel. 01788 5783 28

British Psychological Society (BPS)
St Andrew's House
48 Princess Road East
Leicester
Leics LE1 7DR

tel. 0116 254 9568
fax. 0116 247 0787

Centre for Stress Management
156 Westcombe Hill
London SE3 7DH

tel. (0181) 293 4114
fax. (0181) 293 1441

contact: Stephen Palmer

Institute of Personnel and Development (IPD)
IPD House
Camp Road
London SW19 4UX

tel. (0181) 971 9000
fax. (0181) 263 3333

United States of America

American Association for Adult and Continuing Education (ACCE)
1200 19th Street NW
Suite 300
Washington DC 20036-2401

tel. 202-429-5131
fax. 202-223-4579

Offers magazine, journal and conference

American Management Association (AMA)
PO Box 319
Saranc Lake
MY 12983

tel. 800-262-9699

Offers publications and conference

American Society for Training and Development (ASTD)
1640 King Street
Box 1443
Alexandria
VA 22313
tel.   800-NAT-ASTD (628-2783)
        703-683-8100 Customer service
        703-683-8184 Information center
email. Information Center astdic@capcon.net

Offers local chapters, monthly journal and conference

Centre for Quality Management (CQM)
150 Cambridge Park Drive
Cambridge
MA 02140

tel. 617-873-2152
fax. 617-873-8980

Non-profit clearing-house for quality management and training programs

Institute for Rational Emotive Therapy
Rational Effectiveness Training
45 East Street
New York
NY 10021-6593

contact: Dr DiMattia

tel. 212-535-0822
fax. 212-249-3582

International Personnel Management Association (IPMA)
1617 Duke Street
Alexandria
VA 22314

tel. 703-549-7100

Offers monthly newsletter, quarterly journal and conference

National Association of Government Training and
Development Directors (NAGTADD)
167 West Main Street
Suite 600
Lexington
KY 40507

tel. 606-231-1948
fax. 606-231-1928

National Organizational Development (OD) Network
76 South Orange Avenue
Suite 101
South Orange
New Jersey 07079

tel. 201-763-7337

Offers regional groups, quarterly journal and conferences

Society of Human Resource Management (SHRM)
606 North Washington Street
Alexandria
VA 22314-1997

tel.   800-283-7476
         703-548-3440 membership and information
         703-548-6999 TDD
fax.   703-836-0367
email. shrm@shrm.org

Canada

International Association for Human Resource Information Management
250 Consumers Road
Suite 301
Willowdale
Ontario M2J 4V6

tel. 416-490-6566
fax. 416-495-8723

Ontario Society for Training and Development (OSTD)
110 Richmond Street East
Suite 206
Toronto
Ontario M5C 1P1

tel. 416-367-5900

Offers local chapters, news magazines and conference

Germany

Deutscher Volkshochschulverband
   (German Association of Adult Education)
Fachstelle fuer
Internationale Zusammenarbeit
   (Office of International Cooperation)
Rheinalle 1
D5300 Bonn 2
Germany

Publications

Back, K., Back, K. and Bates, T. (1991) Assertiveness at Work, McGraw-Hill Book Company, Maidenhead.

Bird, M. (1993) *Problem Solving Techniques That Really Work: A step-by-step guide for managers,* Piatkus, London.

de Board, R. (1986) *Counselling Skills,* Wildwood House, Gower, Aldershot.

Burgess, B. (1986) *Problem Solving at Work,* Framework Press, Folens, Dunstable.

Clark, D. and Palmer, S. (1994) *Stress Management,* National Extension College, Cambridge.

Cooper, C., Cooper, R. D. and Eaker, L. H. (1988) *Living with Stress,* Penguin, Harmondsworth.

Dryden, W. and Gordon, J. (1993) *Peak Performance: Becoming More Effective at Work,* Mercury Business Books, Didcot, Oxon.

Myres, D. W. (ed.) (1986) *Employee Problem Prevention and Counselling: A guide for Professionals,* Quorum Books, London.

Palmer, S. (1995) *Stress Management: A quick guide,* Folens, Dunstable.

Reddy, M. (1987) *The Manager's Guide to Counselling at Work,* Methuen, London.

Rickards, T. (1990) *Creativity and Problem Solving at Work,* Gower, London.

Walmsley, H. (1994) *Counselling Techniques for Managers,* Kogan Page, London.

Wheeler, M. (1994) *Problem People at Work and How to Deal with Them,* Century Business, London.

Index